Absent Through Want of Boots

Diary of a Victorian School in Leicestershire

Robert Elverstone

The History Press

Class 2, Hinckley Board School.

First published 2014

The History Press
The Mill, Brimscombe Port
Stroud, Gloucestershire, GL5 2QG
www.thehistorypress.co.uk

British Library Cataloguing in Publication Data.
A catalogue record for this book is available from the British Library.

ISBN 978 0 7509 5218 7

Typesetting and origination by The History Press
Printed in Great Britain

Contents

The New Code of Regulations for 1872 required the Principal Teacher to make an
entry in the logbook at least once each week.

Acknowledgements

I am extremely grateful to Lesley Hagger, Director of Children and Young People's Service in Leicestershire, for granting permission to transcribe extracts from the logbooks of the Hinckley Board Schools. Many thanks to Mrs Cath Allison, head teacher of Holliers Walk Primary School, for allowing access to the books, and to Maggie and Michaela for ensuring their care and survival!

Thank you to the staff of the Record Office for Leicestershire, Leicester and Rutland for their help and support in tracking down information, and especially to Jenny Moran, Senior Archivist (Access and Information), for granting permission to include extracts from the logbooks held in the county collection.

Thanks also to the staff at Chilvers Coton Heritage Centre in Nuneaton for permission to take photographs of their classroom, especially to Rob Everitt for the guided tour. It was very much appreciated.

Many thanks to my wife Julie for help with the pictures and illustrations and for putting up with the hours of research and editing.

A big thank you to all the staff, pupils and parents with whom I had the enormous pleasure to work with for over thirty-five years at this school. And for those whose journey in education is just beginning, especially Eloise and Lizzie, school days are some of the most important in your life. so make good use of them!

Finally, sincere thanks to Mr R.D. Brookes, without whose inspiration this book would never have got started.

Introduction

When Queen Victoria ascended the throne in 1837, education was, at best, an ad hoc affair. Whereas wealthy families could afford to pay for private education, for most of the population schooling was dependent on geographical location and the generosity of local benefactors.

In the early nineteenth century, Sunday schools, charitable schools and ragged schools had all attempted to provide a basic education for children from poorer families.

By 1851, over 17,000 National Schools had been opened by the Church of England. British Schools provided a similar education for children of Nonconformist families.

Some children attended a local Dame School, but there was no formal system of education and no standards by which children's progress could be measured. Neither was there any requirement that children should attend school, many families and employers preferring to keep children working and earning money.

The 1870 Education Act was the first Act of Parliament to pave the way for a compulsory system of National Education for all. The Act placed the responsibility of providing suitable accommodation and teachers firmly in the grasp of local, elected Boards. These schools were known as Board Schools.

The Act gave elected Boards the power to pass by-laws to enforce full-time compulsory education at a local school for all children between the ages of 5 and 10, and for half-time attendance for children up to age thirteen. Boards could charge children 2*d* per week and had the power to prosecute parents who did not ensure the attendance of their children.

School Boards were obliged to ensure there were enough school places for all children in the local area. In Hinckley, this meant the provision of new, purpose-built accommodation.

Victorian schools were generally of red-brick construction with high ceilings. Windows were placed well above the height of children to prevent them being distracted by looking outside. Large rooms to accommodate the children were divided into smaller spaces by hanging curtains.

Each classroom was equipped with a free-standing blackboard and wooden desks placed in rows. Boys and girls were seated separately and, in some schools, in separate classes with their own entrance. The walls would be plain brick, possibly with a poster of Queen Victoria and a map of the British Empire displayed. The teacher would have a desk at the front facing the children. A regime of strict discipline was maintained.

Younger children would each have a slate or sand-tray on which to write. These could be wiped clean and re-used. Older children would write with a pen which was dipped in ink. Left-handed children would be forced to use their right hand to prevent the ink from being smudged.

Class sizes were often huge, up to 100 children in a single class not being uncommon. Because of this, lessons often required copying from the blackboard, rote learning and repetition. Children would be asked to memorise poems, lists of British monarchs and multiplication facts.

Children were able to pass 'standards' which determined which class they were in. With little or no understanding of children with additional needs, this often meant that much older children would find themselves labelled as a 'dunce' and put in a class with much younger children.

Lessons consisted of reading, writing and arithmetic. Once each week an object lesson would take place. The teacher would introduce an object to the classroom and then initiate discussion. In the early days of education, this is as near as most children would ever come to a science lesson.

Boys and girls were taught differently. In addition to basic lessons, girls would be taught needlework while the boys went off to do woodwork. Boys were also taught marching skills, often by a local retired drill sergeant.

Many teachers were unqualified and 'trained' on the job. Children, on leaving school at thirteen, could apply to become pupil teachers. This was a kind of apprenticeship. Pupil teachers received daily lessons from the head teacher. Each year, pupil teachers were examined to see if they could progress to the next year. After five years, these teenagers then qualified as uncertified teachers or assistants. It wasn't until 1946 that government policy required all teachers to be qualified.

Some schools used a monitor system. These were generally older children who assisted the teacher in the classroom. Monitors received additional lessons after school which they would then teach to a small group of younger children the following day. Children who acted as monitors often went on to become pupil teachers.

The school day usually began at nine o'clock with the ringing of the school bell. A midday break was long enough to allow children to go home for dinner and then return in the afternoon. The school day generally finished around half past four or five o'clock.

Children in Hinckley often came from very poor families and, especially in the winter months, were inadequately clothed. The logbooks refer to children being cold or not attending due to poor weather. Particularly in deep snow, some children were marked as absent through 'want of boots'.

Epidemics of measles, scarlet fever and diphtheria were widespread. Lack of medical care and poor health meant these diseases would often lead to death. Ringworm, headlice and 'itch' were common ailments which often caused prolonged absence.

Each year schools were inspected by one of Her Majesty's Inspectors. Inspections would affect teacher salaries and grants for equipment. This 'payment by results' put enormous pressure on the schools to do well, and was partly responsible for the rote learning which the children had to endure.

Head teachers were required to maintain a weekly diary. The logbooks from Hinckley Board School provide a fascinating record of the developments and daily struggles in our local schools. Surprisingly, they also demonstrate that, although some things have undoubtedly changed, for some readers much will be unexpectedly familiar!

Robert Elverstone, 2014

One

Early Days, 1872–1878

In the early days following the 1870 Education Act, the Hinckley Board acquired temporary premises in the congregational church. This allowed time for planning and building the new school.

1872

October 12th: The school was opened on Monday 7th by Mr S.U. Frazer, Certificated Master of the Class One. Several members of the School Board were present and Mr Kiddle, Clerk to the Board, attended for the purpose of enrolling pupils. The week was mainly occupied in organising the school and classifying the pupils. The attendance was very regular and reasonable progress was made. The children seem to be accustomed to but little – if any – homework.

October 19th: The week now ended has been a very busy one. The children were examined, with a view to classification; classes were arranged, details of school routine settled, order and discipline fairly started and satisfactory progress made in actual teaching. By desire of the Board, Mr Frazer undertook the management of the Infant Department until the Board should appoint a Certificated Mistress. Messrs Atkins and Aucott called to consult about books, maps and other apparatus required. The pupil teachers have been punctual and regular and have shown a desire to give satisfaction, which promises well for the future.

November 2nd: Many of the children say that they cannot attend to any home lessons because they have to work all the time they are out of school. In one case, the withdrawal of a pupil was threatened if home lessons of any kind were insisted on.

November 9th: A number of new scholars this week, whose height and age might justify one in assuming some progress in education, do not know the alphabet and can neither write nor figure.

December 20th: School closed for Christmas Holidays, to meet again on December 30th.

December 30th: School reopened after Christmas Holiday, by E. Guilford. Number present at all during week: 27.

1873

January 13th: Numbers fewer in the morning on account of the cattle market in front of the school.

January 20th: First week of competition for attendance prizes with a view to improve the daily attendance. Thirty-eight present at all during week. Children improving in cleanliness.

February 3rd: Attendance poor; wretched weather. The snow very deep on the playground, which prevents the children from coming to school.

February 10th: Fees reduced one penny per week.

February 14th: Twenty-three gained the ticket for regular attendance.

February 25th: A bitter cold morning and snowing fast at nine o'clock which has caused the numbers to be very low. School closed for a half-holiday as it is Shrove Tuesday.

March 5th: Following a request for curtains to separate a group of desks, Mr Farndon and Mr Kiddle visited to take the measurement. During their stay, the children sang several songs and performed various exercises etc. which were much approved and commended to by the gentlemen.

April 4th: Forty-four children gained the blue ticket for regular attendance i.e. had attended ten noons during the week.

April 21st: Sarah Jane Buckler entered on her engagement as pupil teacher. Miss Buckler works satisfactorily, and manages class very well indeed for the first week.

May 21st: Weather very uncomfortable, the rain falling fast all morning, which has caused the attendance to be considerably lower than usual.

June 16th: Highest class examined in numeration and arithmetic, result very fair. Several children away with hooping [*sic*] cough.

July 19th: Number present at all this week 100, highest number attained. Of these, sixty-one gained the regular attendance ticket.

August 22nd: School closed this morning, for a fortnight, on account of the fair etc.

September 8th: School reopened after Harvest Holidays. Sarah Ann Penn entered on her engagement as pupil teacher.

September 18th: Attendance low this morning on account of
Statutes and fair; school closed for a half-holiday
this afternoon.

September 26th: A new set of Royal Prince reading books used this
week, the others being too old for use. A box of
Form and Colour purchased and used. Children
highly delighted with it; but very backward at
finding the colours. Sarah Ann Penn is unable to
obtain a medical certificate, and will therefore be
unable to remain as pupil teacher.

October 17th: School closed for this afternoon, circus in town.

October 27th: Attendance rather lower than last week; several
children absent with blister pox.

November 13th: Sarah Treaddell appointed as pupil teacher by
School Board, duties to commence on Monday,
November 17th.

November 17th: HM Inspectors Report – J.R. Blakiston Esq.:

The infants are in fair order and taught with fair success.
The discipline would be yet more efficient were the
Mistress to cultivate more repose of manner and a more
subdued tone of voice.

The main room being furnished with desks fit only for
older children is not favourable to infants teaching or
management. Some of the desks should be replaced by a
gallery, and the remainder furnished with footboards.

Specimens of needlework should be shown at the
annual examination of scholars. Stocking seaming for
payment is allowed to be done in school hours. As the
By-laws of the School Board make attendance at the
school compulsory, it cannot be urged, as it is in some
adjoining villages, that if forbidden to bring such work,
girls would not attend school. It would seem however that
the By-laws are not enforced, at least many children of

school age are to be seen idling in the streets of the town during school hours.

December 19th: School closed this morning for Christmas Holidays, to reopen January 5th 1874.

Hinckley Board Schools token.

1874

January 12th: Cattle market held in front of school. Youngest children unable to come. Attendance rather low. Two boys sent to the upper school being seven years of age.

January 26th: Laverna Dudley entered on her engagement as pupil teacher.

February 7th: Attendance not as good as last week. Weather very cold and frosty; so severe that several children are unable to come to school.

March 12th: Public examination of children held in the upper room. Infants read and sang several pieces, which gave great satisfaction to a crowded audience. It was proposed and carried 'that the children should have a holiday tomorrow as they had worked so hard before'.

April 4th: School closed this morning for Good Friday and Easter Holidays, to reopen Monday, April 14th.

May 22nd: School closed this morning for a week's holiday (Whitsuntide).

June 19th: Several children away this week with hooping [*sic*] cough.

July 3rd: Attendance good during week until today; circus in the town, attendance low.

July 29th: Attendance rather low this afternoon in consequence of school treats at the Church School.

August 2nd: Two children left in consequence of a child two years old being refused admittance here. The whole family admitted into Church School, no fees being charged for the youngest child.

August 21st: School closed this morning for a fortnight's holiday, to be reopened September 9th 1874.

September 17th: School closed for a half-holiday this afternoon on account of the Statutes and fair.

October 26th: Attendance low today; a menagerie in the town and holiday for stockingers which has kept a number of children at home.

November 17th: Report of HM Inspector J.R. Blakiston Esq.:

The infants are handled and taught with fair success.
The mistress' time should be wholly devoted to
instruction of the infants and a sewing mistress appointed
to take the older girls in needlework. It will be well not to
relax the rule of refusing to admit children less than four
years of age.

The remarks made last year in condemnation of the
practice of allowing seaming to be done in the school, have
been interpreted as expressing approval of the practice.
This and fancy work should forthwith be banished from the
school, and far more attention given to plain needlework,
in which the girls are woefully deficient. A drill sergeant's aid
would be found useful in teaching the boys habits of good
order and prompt obedience.

November 25th: A heavy fall of snow during the night has
considerably lowered the attendance.

December 18th: On account of the inclement state of the weather,
the attendance has been low throughout the week,
especially in the two lowest classes. School closed
this morning for the Christmas Holidays, to be
reopened January 4th 1875.

1875

January 15th: On Monday a cattle market was held close to the
school, which prevented a number of children
coming. Several children promoted from the
lowest class into the third. Teachers and children
worked satisfactorily. Special attention has been
given to the plain sewing.

February 8th: Weather very cold and snow on the ground, which
has reduced the attendance considerably.

February 9th: Shrove Tuesday. School closed for a half-holiday
this afternoon.

March 25th: School closed this morning for the Easter
                     Holidays, to reopen April 5th 1875.

April 29th: E. Guilford, head teacher, sent in her resignation
                     to the School Board.

May 14th: School closed this morning for Whitsuntide
                     Holidays, to reopen Monday May 24th 1875.

June 29th: Entered upon the duties of this school. E.M. West.

July 21st: S.J. Buckler and S. Treaddell had leave of absence
                     this afternoon to attend the children's treat at the
                     Church School. Very few children in consequence
                     of the treat.

August 11th: Too wet for children to go out for play: marching
                     instead. Gave a lesson on 'form' for one of the
                     pupil teachers.

August 16th: Had poetry repeated the last half hour because the
                     children were tired and sleepy.

September 23rd: Half-holiday for the fair.

October 5th: Attendance visitor called; many children away
                     through sickness.

November 4th: Mrs Reeves called for the second time this week
                     to see if her boys were at school as they are
                     continually running away.

November 5th: Mrs Reeves brought her children to school
                     this morning.

November 12th: The new attendance visitor appointed by the
                     Board called in this morning to enquire about a
                     list of irregular children. Mr Kiddle came in with
                     the report of HM Inspector J.R. Blakiston Esq.:

The infants are in nice order and their attainments are very fair. There is room for improvement in lessons on natural history and common things.

Staff	
West, Elizabeth M.	Class Two Headmistress
Dudley, Laverna	4th year Pupil Teacher
Buckler, S. J.	3rd year Pupil Teacher
Treaddell, Sarah	2nd year Pupil Teacher

November 25th: Headmistress sent in resignation to the Board.

December 3rd: Small school owing to a fall of snow during the night – sixty-one present in the morning.

December 15th: Mr Kiddle, Mr Abell and Mr Atkins came in school and heard the children sing.

December 23rd: Closed school this afternoon for the Christmas Holidays.

The teacher's desk stood at the front of the room facing the class. Strict discipline was maintained, the cane being used for even minor infringements. (Photo by permission of Chilvers Coton Heritage Centre)

1876

January 10th: School opened after the Christmas Holidays by
                       K. Ford.

February 14th: Attendance low, forty children present. A deep
                       snow the cause of decrease in numbers.

March 20th: S. Buckley sent by the Board into the third
                       department – Effie Hamson came in place of
                       S. Buckley.

April 3rd: Head teacher absent today – received a letter
                       from the Board stating their acceptance
                       of resignation.

April 28th: Commenced school on Monday after the Easter
                       Holiday. Admitted thirty-four fresh children: the
                       large number admitted is chiefly owing to the
                       closing of Dame School. Found the Class One girls
                       rather backward in needlework – am taking them
                       myself for that subject. Arranged to take the pupil
                       teachers from twelve to one and from four to five in
                       the evening, as they are rather behind their work.

May 6th: Have let the children go out for three or four
                       minutes in the afternoon as the room gets very
                       close by three. Average for the week: 146.

May 13th: On Wednesday two children left in consequence
                       of being reproved for coming dirty. School visited
                       on Thursday by T. Kiddle Esq. who brought the
                       cotton and needles for the knitting. Criticised
                       Miss Dudley's lesson on 'Copper' Thursday
                       afternoon; her language needs care.

May 20th: On Tuesday commenced teaching knitting.
                       The children do not take to it very well.

May 25th: Examined the Class Three in reading; many of them did not know their letters and have sent them back into the classroom. Also examined the little ones and find that though Effie Hamson manages them well and the order is good, still they do not learn much. Have been obliged to forbid the pupil teachers the use of the cane.

June 2nd: Gave the pupil teachers an examination in the work of the last six weeks. The whole of the papers show want of care. The language paper was the best.

June 12th: Opened school this morning after a week's holiday. Attendance fair. The bed for the babies has arrived but is not very large. Admitted five fresh children: was obliged to send two back as they were too young.

June 16th: The children were not able to go out to play Thursday morning, owing to the wet weather. Time spent in singing. Two children came in at ten past three: sent them home again. On Wednesday gave the babies kindergarten instead of counting.

A Victorian headmaster's logbook.

June 24th: Applied this week to the Board for a teacher in the place of E. Hamson, who cannot manage the infants so well, now there are so many.

June 30th: Two children have left this week to go to the Church School in order to go to the treat. Found it advisable to take a class in the playground Wednesday and Thursday as the weather was very hot.

July 5th: A woman came in this morning to complain about her child being ill-used yesterday afternoon. I spoke to Effie about it – was in the room a little before four and found them alright so there must be some mistake. Have noticed a decided improvement in the pupil teachers' work this last fortnight. I spoke to Miss Dudley concerning her behaviour to the children; she is too violent with them.

July 22nd: The attendance this week has been very bad, partly owing to the town cricket match and partly to the school treat. This morning examined the Class One in writing and arithmetic and found they did very well, nineteen out of twenty-five passing. Average for the week: 107.

July 26th: Have been obliged to speak to Miss Treaddell concerning her lessons. She is getting rather careless.

July 31st: Miss Treaddell's lessons badly done again. On Friday gave the pupil teachers an examination in arithmetic, when they passed very well.

August 3rd: Sent in the returns for July to the Board today. Average for the month 133 and the fees amount to £2 8*s*. Miss Treaddell's work has improved since I spoke to her.

August 10th: Left the school in the care of the pupil teachers for the last half hour this afternoon in order to go to a picnic.

August 16th: A woman came this morning and indignantly insisted upon the attendance visitor not being sent after her children as they always came to school. I could not make her understand that in consequence of their so frequently coming after the registers were closed they were marked absent. Miss Buckler complained of the same thing this afternoon. 'If the visitor is sent again, the children will be removed.'

August 19th: Gave an exam to the pupil teachers this week and sent in the papers to the Board. Miss Dudley's history and Miss Treaddell's geography was not well done.

August 23rd: Applied to the Board for a week more holiday, which they have been kind enough to grant.

September 11th: Commenced work again this morning. Miss Miles appointed by the Board as pupil teacher. She is to come a month on trial. Miss Dudley sent word that she had obtained permission from the Board to stay away this week.

September 15th: Have been obliged to deviate a little from the timetable this week, on account of Miss Dudley's absence. So far Miss Miles has proved satisfactory; she is quick and quiet.

September 21st: Attendance not quite as good this morning in consequence of the fair. Half-holiday this afternoon.

September 24th: Attendance not so good in consequence of a circus being in the town.

September 25th: Effie Hamson had permission this afternoon to go to the circus.

September 26th: Gave the pupil teachers a final examination in history and arithmetic. Miss Dudley's carelessly done.

September 27th: Have allowed the Class One girls an extra half an hour of needlework this week in order to finish the work for the exam.

September 29th: Sent several children back today for their school pence.

October 9th: Attendance poor, weather very wet. Children marched during playtime and had a kindergarten game.

October 17th: Was obliged to send one child home again this morning as it was not yet three years old.

October 19th: Miss Dudley away without leave. Wrote to the Board about her.

October 23rd: Miss Dawkins commenced work this morning. She is very intelligent, and seems to manage very well. Commenced fractions and analysis with the pupil teachers.

October 27th: Was obliged to close school this afternoon on account of a circus being in the town.

October 31st: Three more cases of fever; have been obliged to send back one child on account of fever being in the house. Effie Hamson had all the boys yesterday, while the girls were at needlework and managed them very well.

November 2nd: On Monday Miss Treaddell refused to teach history and last night asked the Board to teach it after telling me she would not do so herself. Saw Mr Kiddle this dinnertime about it, and then told her that for the future she must ask me before she goes to the Board.

November 6th: Admitted two fresh children: sent one home again as it was not old enough.

November 10th: Report of HM Inspector J.R. Blakiston Esq.:

The infants are nicely handled and taught with results the more creditable as the premises are unsuitable.

Headmistress	Margaret Westwick	Class Two
Staff	Sarah Treaddell	3rd year Pupil Teacher
	Maria Miles	Monitor
	Joanna Dawkins	Monitor
	Effie Hamson	Candidate

November 15th: Children commenced making their new bags for work this afternoon.

November 17th: Average for the week not so good, many children away with fever and bad eyes.

November 20th: The younger teachers have commenced giving object lessons – find that they all commence by asking questions on the object and questions that the children cannot answer. Also they are satisfied with very little results, only one-third having achieved any good. Took half an hour this dinnertime to go over with them all the chief points in an object lesson.

November 23rd: Yesterday left the pupil teachers in the dinnertime to do their work in consequence of sick headache. Did not find them at all well done, so kept them after school to do lesson again. Attendance not so good today on account of Wombwell's Menagerie being in the town.

December 15th: School visited by Mr Kiddle. The Board have decided to engage Effie Hamson as Candidate.

December 20th: Am leaving the school tomorrow in the care of the pupil teachers. Miss Treaddell will be able to manage them as there are so few, only ninety-seven being present this morning. The school will be closed tomorrow for a week.

Younger children practised writing on a slate or in a sand-tray with their fingers.

1877

January 11th: Have written to the Board for more slates and new books for the Class One. Have determined to prepare the Class One for old first standard.

January 12th: As the children were so cold this morning I changed the second lesson for half an hour's drill.

January 17th: Yesterday the school was visited by Mr Kiddle, who saw the Class One books and allowed me to order fresh ones. Miss Treaddell has commenced her knitting for the examination, and Effie has commenced learning to knit.

January 22nd: Many children away with measles. Children commenced with their new books and will soon be able to read them.

March 6th: Had to speak to Miss Miles about her order; she is getting careless.

March 7th: Since going into the classrooms this week have found the order very bad. Spoke to Effie about it and spoke to all the children about the order. The classes are much larger this week and the order has not been good.

March 13th: Gave the pupil teachers an examination in sums. Miss Miles, Miss Dawkins and Effie passed fairly. Miss Treaddell's all wrong and work carelessly done. The work of the past six months, as regards her sums, has been of very little use.

April 30th: The Board have kindly given me leave for the rest of the week to go to the funeral of my brother in Leeds. The pupil teachers to take the school.

May 17th: Closed school this afternoon for the Whitsuntide Holidays.

June 11th: Admitted six fresh children: was obliged to send one home at half past eleven on account of its crying. Seven children this afternoon came in at three. Punished them and kept them in till five.

June 18th: Attendance not so good; Effie left school at half past eleven to visit some of the absentees and found many of them were ill, chiefly with sore eyes.

June 20th: Spoke to Miss Miles about her order. She has too much to say and will persist on punishing the class.

July 6th: A child left this week for the Church School
in consequence of a sister under three being
refused admittance.

July 11th: School closed this afternoon in consequence of
the Church School Treat.

August 24th: School closed for a week on account of the fair.

September 12th: Effie Hamson absent this morning to attend an
examination held at the Town Hall.

September 13th: Miss Treaddell gave a lesson on 'Milk' to upper
section this afternoon. Allowed too many to play.

Girls had to learn needlework. This piece was prepared for
an examination.

September 20th: Miss Treaddell's work very carelessly done this
                  week and the old excuse offered; 'She has forgotten.'
                     Notwithstanding the fact that hooping [*sic*]
                  cough is prevalent in the town; the average this
                  week has been very good: 172. On Tuesday
                  afternoon the school was closed owing to the fair.

September 24th: Have arranged with Mrs Webb at the Church
                  Infant School to receive no children who have
                  made their times from this school. During the
                  last month, Miss Treaddell has received two hours
                  instruction at English besides the two hours daily,
                  owing to her general backwardness.

October 12th: Average attendance still poor. Many children away
                  with coughs and colds. On Tuesday was obliged to
                  send two children home with hooping [*sic*] cough.

October 18th: Annual Examination by J.R. Blakiston. School
                  closed this afternoon.

November 5th: Admitted two fresh children – was obliged to send
                  three home with hooping [*sic*] cough and two
                  with sore hands.

November 8th: This morning a boy came in at twelve covered from
                  head to foot with clay. Gave him the cane and should
                  have kept him in but as his sisters came, allowed him
                  to go. In twenty minutes his father came, using very
                  bad language and threatening an 'action'.
                     Miss Treaddell gave a lesson on 'Bark' to
                  upper section. Order not very good. Gave words
                  which the class did not understand without
                  any explanation.

November 16th: Have received notice from Mr Kiddle that the
                  Board have decided to engage Mary Wright to
                  take the place of Miss Treaddell, who will be
                  transferred to the upper school.

November 30th: In consequence of there being a few soldiers in the town, attendance not so good this morning.

December 21st: School closed this morning for the Christmas Holidays.

December 31st: School opened this morning. S. Treaddell commenced duty in the upper room. Mary Wright, who was to have taken her place, was away ill. Applied for S. Treaddell to come back, but a girl was sent.

1878

January 1st: Do not find the monitors sufficient, a fresh one being sent every time. Am obliged to send a senior in to help them. Admitted two fresh children and filled in the government certificates.

January 11th: This morning a woman came and refused to pay her child's school pence any longer. Referred her to the Board.

January 18th: Mary Wright has completed one week of her month on trial. Find her very quick and deficient in order. She has been in the babies' room all week.

February 1st: School visited by Mr Kiddle who advised me to write to the Board and apply for another teacher as Mary Wright is not suitable and she seems so little adapted for school work.

February 4th: This afternoon sent a child back for her money as there were two weeks owing for. When the mother came, and after a deal of abusive language, she refused to pay the school pence.

February 5th: Holly Goode at school this morning without her
pence. Sent her home this afternoon for it and
refused to have her till it is sent.

March 5th: Shrove Tuesday. School closed in consequence.

March 18th: Admitted two fresh children and two returned
who have been away all winter.

March 25th: Severe snow storm. Very few children here.
Miss Miles took the Class Three with the
babies and Miss Dawkins the first and second.
Allowed Miss Wright, who came at ten,
to go back home as she seemed very weak.
Miss Hamson employed at needlework as it is
her worst subject.

March 29th: School visited by Mr Kiddle, who told me that
the Board had raised my salary. Have taken the
pupil teachers for lessons in the dinnertime all this
week and allowed Miss Dawkins to leave at 3.30
as her mother still continues very ill. Average for
week: 131.

April 4th: Letter from Miss Dawkins this morning; her
mother died last night. In consequence she will
not return to school this week. Applied to Board
for books for Class Three and two reading boards.

April 11th: On Monday admitted five fresh children and
three, who were transferred last week, have
returned, not yet being seven. Miss Dawkins sent
in her resignation; she wishes to leave in a month.

April 19th: School closed this afternoon for the Easter
Holidays, to be reopened April 29th.

April 30th: Mary Wright obliged to go home ill. Has sent in
to the Board her resignation.

May 16th: Allowed the pupil teachers ten minutes this morning
                   to see a wedding. E. Hamson gave an object lesson
                   to the upper section this afternoon. As the lesson had
                   not been prepared it was badly given.

May 17th: Mary Wright's notice expires this week, but as we
                   have not yet been able to engage another in her
                   place, I have asked her to come for a few more days.

May 24th: E. Hamson went after absentees today. Many
                   away with colds.

May 28th: Refused the admittance of two children today, not
                   yet being three.

June 7th: Examined the first and Class Twos on Monday
                   and found them fairly proficient. On Wednesday
                   examined the third and was obliged to speak
                   strongly to Maria with regard to the reading and
                   writing work, it being very poor. Mary Wright has
                   agreed to stay to the end of the quarter as we have
                   been unable to engage another one yet. School
                   closed today for a fortnight on account of the
                   Whitsuntide Holidays.

July 2nd: Miss Riddington commenced her month on trial.
                   Appears to be rather quick.

July 10th: School closed today on account of the Church
                   School Treat.

July 11th: Sent in to the Board the returns for last month.
                   Also a list of children whose fees are in arrears and
                   whose parents refuse to pay.

July 16th: School visited by Mr Kiddle who brought the
                   list of children to be remitted by the Board with
                   one exception, if the fees have been brought
                   this afternoon.

July 22nd: Admitted three children and had to refuse two on
                      account of being too young.

July 26th: Had to speak to Miss Miles and Miss Riddington
                      about the order in their classes, which is very
                      poor. With the exception of the Class One, all the
                      children are beginning to show the effects of being
                      too long without a teacher.

August 6th: Examined the pupil teachers today.
                      Miss Riddington has made very little progress,
                      being quite unable to revise or do practice.
                      She also shows very little improvement in
                      teaching, being altogether too lax with the class.

August 16th: Have been obliged to take the Class Three from
                      Miss Miles as the class learns absolutely nothing.

August 22nd: Wrote to the Board, urging the necessity of at
                      once engaging a teacher.

August 24th: School closed this morning for a week, on account
                      of the fair. Packed up all the school apparatus to be
                      taken up to the new schools.

Hinckley Board School opened on September 2nd 1878.
Designed by R.J. & J. Goodacre of Leicester, and built by
T. & G. Harrold, it was one of the largest Board Schools
in Leicestershire.

Two

New Beginnings, 1878–1881

The schools in temporary accommodation closed on August 24th 1878 in order to transfer apparatus to the newly built school in Albert Road.

1878

September 2nd: Commenced work at the new schools with 245 children. Admitted forty-seven fresh ones and had several old ones retained. Did not quite keep to the timetable as people were constantly coming in and out. At a quarter before twelve several gentleman who are on the Board came in and heard the children sing. W.G. Farmer Esq. spoke to them about the school and they were then dismissed with a holiday for the rest of the day.

September 18th: Mr Grimble came this afternoon with a complaint that his boy had been made to stand on one leg and had been beaten on the back of his hand with the cane. As no such thing had occurred, called out the boy who then said it was a boy from the upper school who had done it coming home. The man appeared quite satisfied with the information.

September 22nd: Attendance very fair this week – it being very cold and many of the children are away with colds.

1879

May 14th: Very wet and cold. Attendance poor.

May 15th: Last night a man, Mr Jennings, came to my
rooms with his little girl and affirmed that her
head had been marched against the wall by Effie
(pupil teacher). There was a large swelling on
the back of the child's head. This morning, on
questioning, Effie claimed she knew nothing
about it and the child then said it was one of the
other children. Sent for the mother and satisfied
her as to the blame.

July 1st: Took charge of this, the Hinckley Board Infants'
School. Signed: E. Hill, Certificated Class Two.
Found the school in a most unsatisfactory condition
as regards order. The Girls, Standard One and infants
have not even commenced a specimen piece, garment,
or knitting for the examination – there is not any of
this year's needlework in the school.

July 2nd: Examined Standard One in arithmetic this
morning. Thirty-nine were in class, four of whom
passed – more than two-thirds could not take
numbers up to hundreds from dictation.

July 4th: Examined Class One of infants. They are backward
in reading and notation – fair in writing. The pupil
teachers have done very little of their examination
needlework – the little that is done, is dirty and
badly done. The last quarter's registers, which
Miss Nestwick should have made up, are left undone.

July 12th: Sent teachers after two in arrears.

July 14th: Punished several children for coming after the
registers were marked this afternoon.

July 19th: Sent home Clara Shipman as her brother has scarlatina. Alfred and Eliza Newton have gone to the Church School because refused to take them back until all danger of infection from scarlatina was over.

September 8th: The timetable cannot be strictly followed with while the teaching staff is short. It is impossible to get the school into good working order while the teachers are constantly away.

September 12th: Gave list of absentees to attendance visitor yesterday. Two boys came in at half past three this afternoon. Several caps have been taken from the cloakroom this week. The girls have not had any needlework this week. Mistress has taken full charge of Class Two all the week. The children are very dull and inattentive – but are gradually getting into better order.

September 29th: Examined Class One today. Notation slightly improved, but still very difficult. Reading very, very backward. The greatest progress has been made in writing.

September 30th: Examined Class Two today. Decided improvement in notation and order, but attainments are still very much below what they should be.

October 9th: Martha and Mary Smith are away with scarlatina. Millie Jones, who was at school yesterday week, is to be buried this afternoon. She died during an attack of scarlatina.

October 10th: Mistress absent this afternoon. Registers marked and school conducted by the assistant and pupil teachers. Gave list of absentees and arrears to attendance visitor.

October 16th: George Smith died this morning from scarlatina. He was at school a week today.

October 17th: Drill and singing are the two last lessons on the timetable for Friday afternoons. For the future the classes will take the same lesson as on Monday afternoon from three to half past three and singing until four. Children in the Class One have begun to learn singing from the Tonic-So-Fah [*sic*] system.

November 4th: Another scholar, Arthur Brown, died last evening. Attendance visitor called for absentee list. Miss Dudley late again this morning. Have constantly to remind her that she should be here not later than five to eight and five to two.

November 5th: Pupil teachers' home lessons not known this morning – will be required to remain after twelve.

November 13th: Florence Griffin, from Class Three, died yesterday. Several children still absent with scarlatina.

November 14th: Sent Sam Richards on home this morning for coming after the registers were marked. Attendance has been low all the week. Sent after absentees and arrears.

November 18th: Punished several children for coming in school after the registers were marked this afternoon.

November 19th: Miss Dudley arrived at half nine this morning.

November 25th: Number present small owing to snow storm. Third and Class Fours taken together in babies' room. Effie did needlework all the morning – she is very backward in that subject. Arthur Turnbull absent through scarlatina in the family.

November 27th: Sent after absentees. Taught children 'Lightly Fall'.

November 30th: Very small school owing to severe weather.
Fred Bedford from Class Three died yesterday
from scarlatina. The monthly exam should have
taken place this week, but have deferred till next
week owing to bad attendance.

This inkwell was in use until 1959. It held three bottles of ink:
black, red and copier. Copier ink was used to make copies by
applying wet tissue to the completed writing. This gave a mirror
image so it had to be held up to the light and read from the back.

1880

January 22nd: Attendance visitor returned absentee list. A large
number still away through illness. Sent letter to
Board asking for some pegs in the babies' room as
the babies are often losing their hats etc.

January 23rd: Received new sewing materials. Attendance
gradually improving. Average for the week: 169.9.

January 27th: School visited by Mr Kiddle. Children took
singing for the last lesson instead of lessons on
the timetable.

January 28th: Punished several children who came in after the registers were marked.

January 29th: Received notice this morning of the Pupil Teacher Examination to be held on Saturday next at Nuneaton.

January 30th: The new school year closes today.

February 5th: Sent the following report to Board:

Average for month	= 173
Number on Roll	= 231
Money paid in	= £2 7s 3d

Asked for cupboard for babies' room and new locks on cupboard and drawers in centre room.

February 6th: Several children came after registers were closed: kept them after the others had gone.

February 9th: John and Elizabeth Griffin returned today after four months absence through scarlatina.

February 10th: Examined Class One. Notation fairly good. Writing and dictation fair. Reading improving. Half-holiday given today as it is Shrove Tuesday.

February 11th: Miss Dudley absent today with a headache.

February 12th: Examined Class Two today. Miss Miles has taken real pains with her class. The improvement is very decided, although some few are very backward and need great individual attention. Effie's class shows careful teaching especially in notation.

Spoke seriously to Miss Dudley about staying away from school unless really ill – also of her carelessness on coming so often late.

February 23rd: Admitted several new children – one girl, Katie
                     Armstrong, six years of age, does not know her letters.

February 25th: Gave certificates to all children in Standard One
                     who passed in all three subjects.

March 11th: Willie Harvey and Richard Griffin have played
                     truant this week; the former several times.

March 12th: The attendance is better again this week.
                     Miss Dudley has received notice that she has
                     passed her Certificate Examination and is placed
                     in the third division.

March 15th: Sent after absentees. Punished several children
                     who came in after the registers were closed. Willie
                     Harvey away. A coach went over him last week
                     while playing truant.

March 17th: Willie Harvey returned to school. Miss Dudley
                     taught the children a new song 'The Grass'.

March 23rd: Report of HM Inspector Revd Capel:

                     Discipline and fitness for training apprentices good.
                     The children above seven did moderately in reading, fairly
                     in dictation and arithmetic.
                         The infants did fairly in reading and dictation and
                     moderately in arithmetic. The needlework is fair.
                         M. Miles and E.A. Hamson have passed well and
                     S.A. Riddington fairly.

Staff	
Emily Hill	Headmistress Class Two
Laverna Dudley	Assistant Mistress
Maria Miles	Pupil Teacher 4th year
Effie Hansom	Pupil Teacher 3rd year
Sarah Riddington	Pupil Teacher 3rd year

April 7th: Half-holiday today on account of County Election.

April 8th: Small school this afternoon owing to public demonstration result of yesterday's election.

April 12th: Teachers commence lessons at seven in the morning this week.

April 15th: Sent following report to Board for month ending March:

Numbers on roll	= 256
Average for month	= 198
Fees	= £2 8s 6d
Money for needlework	= £1 3s 4d

April 16th: Sent after absentees and arrears.

April 20th: Mr Foxwell visited school today. Took down the number in each class. The classes are all too large for the teachers; especially Miss Riddington's who often has seventy children to teach.

May 14th: As the children throughout the school came so late, have made a rule that all children in Classes One, Two and Three shall be punished who came in after ten past nine in the morning and ten past two in the afternoon.

May 15th: Very few children late today. Three came in after the registers were closed.

May 18th: Punished Susan and Sarah Jane Knight for playing truant several times this week. Sent after absentees and arrears.

May 21st: The seats of the desks have been altered and made more comfortable. Footboards have also been added.

May 30th: Examined Class Two. Reading and notation have improved. Writing is the best subject. Tables very poor. Effie has her new class rather more under control than at first. Next month's books will show more decided improvement I trust.

May 31st: Morning examined Class Three as it was Miss Riddington's first month with class. No very decided advance made.

July 5th: Punished John Mason for playing truant this morning by locking him in till half past six this evening.
　　Miss Howkins came this morning to see how she can get on with teaching.

July 6th: Miss Dudley came this morning for the first time to help with the pupil teachers.

July 7th: Owing to heavy storm only 214 present this morning.

July 9th: Sent attendance visitor after arrears.

July 13th: Ada and Frank Marshall have spent their school money for several weeks – their arrears were paid today.
　　Emmeline Harries is getting on very well with her class. She is a bright, careful little teacher.
　　Annie Howkins shouts and stamps too much in teaching. Have already cautioned her several times – she tries to overcome the habit.

July 16th: Children very troublesome today owing to the heat. Taught children words of a new marching song.

July 19th: Several mothers have tried to get their children admitted under three years of age, but will not take them.

July 20th: Timetable not strictly adhered to in Effie and
Annie Howkins' absence. Very large attendance
this afternoon: 272 present. Found considerable
difficulty in managing without the two absent
teachers. Miss Dudley's order is very poor.

July 22nd: A holiday given today on account of the Church
School Treat.

July 26th: A terrific storm about two o'clock this afternoon,
by which the place was flooded, prevented the
children from coming to school, so that we closed
for the afternoon.

Miss Howkins has decided not to remain –
she does not like the book, it is too hard for her.

Find it very inconvenient to have four classes
working together in the large room, but the
apparatus and seat accommodation is too badly
arranged in Classroom One to admit Class Two
being there; otherwise the room is large enough.

August 30th: School reopened this morning. Headmistress absent.
School conducted by assistant and pupil teachers.

September 2nd: Sent monthly returns to Board – average for
month: 255 – a considerable decrease owing
principally to the Church School Treat and
the fair. Several children absent this week with
measles. Weather intensely hot. Children very
sleepy and troublesome.

September 6th: Effie Hamson absent from lessons this morning
through illness. Two mothers came with children
under three years of age wanting admission for
them but were refused.

September 7th: John Bedford played truant this afternoon.
Received a dozen new dusters today, together with
new needlework materials.

Take Misses Wells, Riddington and Harris for reading a short time extra each every day as they are such poor readers. Effie Hamson tries very hard with her needlework but is still a very poor worker. Locked Fred Burton in the babies' room for half an hour after the others had gone as he is such a very troublesome boy.

September 16th: Sent letter to the Board suspecting Miss Wells, who has passed her month of probation, that I think her capable of performing the duties of a Candidate.

Received from one of the parents that Miss Dudley has sent children out of school on objectionable errands without my knowledge. Have given orders that no child is to be sent out of school under any circumstances or pretext what-so-ever.

September 30th: Sent report to Board and asked to have some forms printed to send to parents whose children fail to bring their school money.

October 1st: The average for this week is much lower than the previous week owing to the measles.

October 27th: Emmeline Harris gave her first singing lesson this afternoon. Found that Mary Parkin and Emmeline Harris have been in the habit of staying at school until one o'clock to do their home lessons. Have forbidden them to do so as it is too long a time to be in school from eight till one o'clock.

October 29th: Locked John Huckle in the classroom all the dinner hour for playing truant yesterday. Have cautioned Mary Parker about being late to lessons in the morning.

November 2nd: Received six dozen new slates.

1881

January 10th: School reopened this morning after Christmas Holidays. Miss Legge, ex-pupil teacher of the Gillingham Board Infants' School, commenced duty as Assistant Mistress today.

January 11th: Too cold and snowy today for the children to go out to play – had marching and singing instead.

January 12th: The order of the babies' room needs improving – Miss Wells is exceedingly noisy in her manner of teaching.

January 24th: Weather not improved, attendance very poor. Sent after absentees. Board have cancelled arrears to the end of the school year. Gave the pupil teachers a final examination on Saturday. Mary Wells' and Mary Parker's arithmetic papers were both carelessly worked. Miss Riddington's grammar poor.

The 1881 census shows the Board School House being occupied by William Heaton and his wife Susannah (certified teachers), their four sons (scholars), Annie Daffeen (pupil teacher) and Elizabeth Hodges (general servant). The small hole in the wall beside the door was to scrape muddy boots.

January 26th: Examined Miss Riddington's class. A few bright children but the most of them are rather dull and backward.

March 1881: Report of HM Inspector:

This school is improving steadily – I believe Miss Hill will make it a very good one.

Effie Hamson has passed well and S. Riddington fairly.

Staff	
Emily Hill	Headmistress
Harriet Legge	Assistant
Effie Hansom	4th year Pupil Teacher
Sarah Riddington	4th year Pupil Teacher
Mary Parker	1st year Pupil Teacher
Mary Wells	Monitor
Emmeline Mary Harris	Monitor

March 25th: Effie Hamson unable to come today – cannot keep to timetable with only three monitors to help.

March 28th: Messrs Foxwell and Atkins called this morning to make arrangements about staff, but came to the conclusion that it would be unwise to have temporary assistants because of the scarlatina. Misses Legge, Riddington and Hamson all away.

April 1st: The Board decided last evening to make Mary Parker a pupil teacher and to continue Mary Emmeline Harris and Mary Wells as monitors.

The girls have not had sewing this week – the timetable has been kept to as far as possible, but it has been impossible to adhere to it strictly.

April 4th: Miss Riddington returned this morning after six weeks absence. Misses Legge and Dawson still too ill to be present.

Monitors were employed to help in the classrooms. One of
their jobs was to mix the ink each morning and top up the
inkwells in the children's desks. (Photo by permission of
Chilvers Coton Heritage Centre)

April 7th: Mary Emmeline Harris sent to say she is unable
to come to school as a kettle of hot water fell on
her leg. Three teachers away again. It is impossible
to conduct the school properly in their absence.

April 8th: The school will close today for a fortnight instead
of one week's holiday on account of the illness of
the teachers.

April 26th: Miss Wells (monitor) objected to pick up a few
pieces of paper and to swap a few bits of coal into
the stove on the ground that it was not her place
to do such work. She did it eventually but said she
should not come again, so she was told to put her
hat on and go home at once.

In the course of the afternoon Mrs Wells came
and spoke very strongly on the subject of her
daughter having to do such menial work as that
and putting coal into the stoves too.

I told Mrs Wells that that kind of work was
obliged to be done by the teachers when necessary
and if her daughter objected to doing it she had
better give up the thought of being a teacher.

Mrs Wells left and returned shortly afterwards to say she would try to persuade Polly (Mary) to return if I would not mention the subject again for her.

I refused to have her at school again unless she apologised.

April 27th: Miss Wells came to say she was sorry for her misconduct yesterday. I have allowed her to return on condition that she be willing to take her share of any and all the work required to be done.

April 28th: Copy of letter received from Board concerning Miss Wells:

Dear Miss Hill,

The Board requires the junior teachers and monitors under your superintendence to do any domestic work you desire necessary for the comfort and cleanliness of the schools, being assured you will not require what is not either necessary or reasonable.

Yours Truly
(signed) T. Kiddle

May 4th: Mistress came to school but obliged leave because of illness.

May 16th: Mistress absent since May 4th returned today. School has been carried on by the assistant and pupil teachers.

July 8th: The attendance very much smaller this week owing to one or two wet days. Girls commenced their examination needlework.

July 11th: Several of the parents came respecting their arrears, as the Board have sent out notices to the effect that unless the arrears are paid they will be summoned before the County Court.

July 17th: Allowed Miss Legge to leave early as she has lost her voice.

August 5th: Miss Wells away ill again today. Miss Legge still too weak to attend.

August 10th: Gave half-holiday this afternoon because of the County Agricultural Show held here.

August 11th: Another half-holiday this afternoon.

August 12th: A cold, wet morning. Only 169 children present.

August 15th: Received the school harmonium.

Hinckley Board School logbook in use until October 1905. The lock was engineered by Windle and Blythe.

August 23rd: Very wet, stormy day, only 149 children
present (afternoon). Gave the pupil teachers an
examination on Friday evening. The papers were,
most of them, carefully written, the weakest
subjects being arithmetic and history.

August 25th: Closed school this morning for the Fair Holiday.

October 21st: Gave the pupil teachers a written examination on
Saturday last. The most unsatisfactory papers were
Mary Parker's arithmetic and geography.

Examined the whole school individually
this week – the four-year-old children seem to
have suffered most through the smallness of the
staff. There are a large number of six-year-old
children who are very backward and need much
individual attention.

Three

Golden Jubilee, 1882–1888

Queen Victoria's Golden Jubilee is celebrated on 20th and 21st June 1887 with a holiday. Absenteeism and unpaid fees continue to be major problems.

1882

February 1st: I, Annie Lees, Class Two Certificate Teacher, took charge of this school. The attendance has been very poor, owing doubtless to the fact of there having been a day's holiday. Sent up Standard One to the mixed department and re-classified children.

February 6th: Have given a list of absentees to the Board attendance visitor this afternoon; have also admitted several new scholars. Pupil teacher lessons will for the present be carried on from quarter to eight until ten to nine.

February 20th: Punished six boys who came in after the registers were closed this afternoon. Emmeline Harris bids fair to be a good teacher. Stopped work for fifteen minutes this morning for the purpose of having strict order maintained throughout the school.

February 21st: School will be closed this afternoon it being Shrove Tuesday.

February 28th: Gave Board attendance visitors list of irregulars. Sarah Riddington absent this morning on business connected with the Scholarship Examination. Mary Parker gave a lesson on 'The Spider'.

March 28th: Annie E. Knight reprimanded this morning on the 'old grievance'; no lessons prepared. The order in Class Two girls decidedly better yesterday and today. Polly Wells has no control whatever over the children. Whichever class she takes is sure to be fidgety and disorderly. It is to be hoped she will very soon improve.

March 30th: Sent Ada Goddard home for her money yesterday and the day before. This morning received note from her mother which stated that she will not pay what is owing. Further saying that if Ada were sent home again she would be kept until sent after. She was accordingly sent back home with a message for her mother to come up and set matters straight which had no effect.

May 19th: Annie E. Knight absent from lessons this morning, excuse: indisposition. A child sent home ill this afternoon. Several children are away from school ill: scarlet fever is prevalent.

May 22nd: Polly absent from lessons this morning. She is leaving this week, and has asked that her attendance at lessons may be excused as she is working up for an Examination in Music, and would be glad of the time to devote to it.

June 26th: Mistress absent from lessons this morning through illness. The timetable has not been strictly followed this afternoon, owing to a mistake of one of the pupil teachers.

June 30th: Lily Kiddle been absent since Monday, bypermission, to go to the seaside.

At ten o'clock this morning Mary Parker sent home because she was told to take a lower class than ordinarily. Shortly after her mother came up. After an explanation Mary came back.

Sarah Riddington left school this afternoon at half past three, by permission. The Scholarship Examination commences on Monday next, consequently she will be away from school. Permission has been granted for her to stay in London during the following week also.

Another complaint has been made this week about Annie E. Knight beating the children. She has to be constantly told of it.

July 5th: Mary Parker reprimanded this afternoon for striking a child. One of the babies fell off the bed this morning and bruised its forehead. It has not been possible to strictly follow the timetable during the absence of Sarah and Lily.

Report to Board for July is as follows:

Roll	= 354
Highest present	= 269
Average	= 243.8
Fees	= £5 5s 1d

The Admission Register shows an increase of 100 scholars since February 1st 1882.

August 3rd: Sent home two children who have ringworm this afternoon.

August 8th: A woman came this morning about her boy's cap which has been lost and threatened not to pay any school money until she has taken full value of it (the cap).

August 10th: The attendance during the last few weeks has
                     been considerably lower owing partly, no doubt,
                     to scarlatina, which is prevalent among children.

August 21st: On Saturday last, Mrs Goode (mother of one of the
                     pupils) complained of the bad treatment her child
                     had received on Friday afternoon from its teacher.
                     It had gone home with its clothes saturated with
                     water which had been thrown over it. It was found
                     this morning, upon the investigation of the affair,
                     that three of the teachers were guilty. They were
                     reprimanded very severely and also told what the
                     consequences would be, did such a thing ever
                     occur again.

                     At nine o'clock Mrs Wills sent a letter stating
                     that 'Her little Grace [one of the offenders] was so
                     upset at what had been said to her that she would
                     not be able to come to school all day.' Consequently
                     she was absent. The letter further went on to say she
                     (Mrs Wills) was hoping so much would not have
                     been said. She had said enough herself, evidently
                     considering that the Mistress ought not to correct
                     the girl for bad conduct in school.

1883

May 28th: Miss Scanlon absent with ringworm. All the other
                     teachers present.

November 9th: On Wednesday morning from nine o'clock to
                     nine forty the children had marching instead
                     of the ordinary scripture lesson – on account of
                     the weather being cold. Miss Scanlon is leaving
                     having obtained an Assistantship under the
                     Leicester School Board.

November 16th: Headmistress absent from lessons on Monday
                     morning owing to the cold weather. During this

week, the children have (on most mornings) spent
about ten or fifteen minutes exercising first thing.
The children this week have finished learning words
and tune of 'There's a Friend for Little Children'.
In spite of cold and dull weather, the attendance has
been for the most part very good.

November 19th: Miss Scanlon was liberated by the Board on
Saturday. The vacancy, thus caused, is as yet
unfilled. The changes caused by both the assistant
teachers leaving cannot but be detrimental,
in some degree, to the good of the school.

This unusual object was used for drawing five parallel lines
on the blackboard. The scissor action meant that the distance
between the lines could be altered. (Photo by permission of
Chilvers Coton Heritage Centre)

1884

September 29th: Beatrice Pickering is absent through illness.
A note has been received (by Mistress) from her
father, to the effect that medical advice has been
obtained and that while she will probably be able
to attend school tomorrow, it will be absolutely
necessary that she does no studying whatever
for the next fortnight. She is suffering from
nervous debility.

October 3rd: The first, second and Class Threes have been
                     examined this week. Some of the children in
                     Standard One are very quick but there are
                     several backward ones who pull down the
                     percentage very perceptively. The Class Two
                     boys did very well, the percentage being 90.
                     There was also visible improvement in the
                     Class Two girls. The Class Three children
                     seemed to have great difficulty in mastering
                     their addition.

October 7th: Beatrice Pickering is away with rheumatic fever.

October 24th: A boy was punished this morning for taking
                     the wrong cap out of the cap room yesterday.
                     Misses Carryer and Sarll have given model
                     lessons to the second and Class Threes on
                     'How the earth is natured' and 'The Mouth'.
                     Both maintained good order and gave very
                     fair lessons.

November 14th: The pupil teachers' lessons this week and last have
                     been superintended by Misses Carryer and Sarll.
                     The Headmistress has not arrived at school until
                     about half past nine this week.

November 21st: It was decided at the Board meeting last night
                     that two weeks holiday should be given this
                     Christmas instead of the usual one week, on
                     account of Christmas Day falling on Thursday.
                     The attendance this week has not been so high,
                     owing probably to the dull, cold weather.

1885

January 27th: Annie E. Knight has been censured this morning
                     for striking a child. She has, of late, been careless
                     again in that respect.

February 13th: There are several children away with whooping cough.

February 16th: This afternoon the children were examined in singing by S.F. Tomline Esq.

March 2nd: Took charge of this, the Hinckley Board Infants' School. Signed: S. Slater Certificated (Class Two).

March 5th: Miss Carryer asked permission to be absent from school today, in order to meet the members of a School Board. The pupil teachers come to lessons at eight o'clock instead of eight thirty.

March 6th: Many children absent today owing to the inclemency of the weather. Second and Class Threes took singing instead of kindergarten this afternoon.

April 15th: 1885 Inspection Report:

The infants did very fairly in reading and well in dictation and arithmetic. The object lessons are quite up to the average. The singing is satisfactory and so is the needlework; a beginning has been made with kindergarten work. The discipline is hardly equal to the instruction, and the quality of the reading may easily be improved.

The average attendance in the infants' department must not exceed the number for which the plans were approved by this department viz. 251 or the entire grant to that department will be endangered.

May 1st: Forty-three boys and thirty-five girls have been sent into other schools today in order to reduce the average in this department. Those children who are not fit for the standard are retained and will work with the six-year-old children.

Annie E. Knight has been transferred to the girls' department and Maud Hugill leaves today.

Her place is taken by Maud Winfield.
In consequence of these changes, the classes will
be rearranged and the routine slightly altered.
Miss Carryer will take the babies instead of
Edith Wells (pupil teacher).

July 6th: A little boy named William Payne in the baby
class fell down in the playground this morning
and broke his arm. It was quite an accident and
so no one was to blame. The child's sister was
sent home and the grandfather came down to
school. He seemed quite perfectly satisfied with
my explanation and took the child to the doctor.
I have instructed the teachers to watch their
classes well when they are in the playground.

School closed at eleven thirty this morning.
Half-holiday given on account of Church
School Treat.

July 9th: Attendance poor all day. It was very warm in the
afternoon and the children were very restless
during the needlework lesson.

September 17th: A half-holiday given this afternoon because of
the Statutes.

September 18th: Have examined all the classes this week and find
the children throughout are slowest in mental
arithmetic. There is great improvement in reading,
especially in the Class Two, and writing is very
satisfactory. The teachers keep their classes in
better order.

December 8th: School closed this afternoon on account of the
Parliamentary Elections.

December 11th: Attendance poor this week owing to the
inclement weather. Average for the week: 248.
Children now spend the time from nine o'clock

to half past nine in marching. Heard the pupil teachers give lessons during the week and noticed improvement in each case.

December 18th: Miss Everitt has taught the children a new action song this week viz. 'The Little Soldier'.

The bell was rung at the beginning of each school session and in the classroom to maintain order, particularly in large classes. It was also used as a fire alarm.

1886

March 9th: School closed for half-holiday, it being Shrove Tuesday.

March 12th: A little extra time has been devoted to singing lately, preparing for the concert to be held next Thursday.

March 18th: No school this morning – entertainment in the afternoon and school closed for part of week.

March 22nd: Admitted six new scholars in the morning. So few children present in the afternoon on account of a circus being in town that registers were not marked and children sent back.

March 26th: Have examined all the classes this week and find children are making fair progress in their work, but the order is not very good in any of the classes, which is owing to the many interruptions since the examination.

October 15th: Very few children present this afternoon – the weather being wet and stormy. One or two of the teachers have been doing their examination needlework. The school is very crowded now. Average for week: 311.

October 27th: Mrs Everitt has taught the children one or two new songs. Have heard the pupil teachers give object lessons and gave them an examination last Saturday. Maud Winfield's papers were carelessly done.

November 2nd: Miss Everitt left school at half past two this afternoon. The children in her class are very dull and attend badly. This morning I examined the class, and although Miss Everitt has worked well with them, the results were unsatisfactory.

November 26th: The order has not been very good lately. Florence Lees' class is especially noisy. Miss Everitt has taught the children a new song viz. 'The Poppies'. Many of the younger children attend very irregularly just now.

December 1st: Mistress away from school this morning, in order to attend the annual audit of the school books. Edith gave a Bible lesson yesterday morning. It was a great improvement upon the last and her manner was pleasing and interesting.

December 9th: Have examined the various classes this week. The work is very satisfactory. Grace Wells has taken great pains with the dunces. Many of them have made great progress, so I have placed them in the second division of Class Three. As five classes have to work in the schoolroom, and sometimes the numbers are high, work is not carried on as quietly as it otherwise would be.

1887

February 23rd: Yesterday being Shrove Tuesday, a half-holiday was given. Harriet Wills absent this morning: she is suffering from a bad cold and unfit to attend school.

March 4th: The children who were sent up to the other departments have been in several times this week to practise for a concert to be held in a week or two. More time has been given to singing lately on that account. This causes children to be somewhat unsettled and the order has been very poor all week.

March 14th: It was decided at the Board meeting held Friday last that Harriet Wills and Lily Haughton act as Candidates on Probation this year. Attendance poor this morning owing to the severe weather. Miss Carryer has gone home this morning.

March 15th: Called over the registers of Class Three first and second divisions in the new building and found them correct. (Signed) T. Kiddle, Clerk.

March 16th: The annual entertainment will be held tomorrow
afternoon, in consequence of which school closes
today for the rest of the week. Miss Carryer has
been absent since Monday, being too ill to fulfil
her duties. The attendance in the babies' school has
been very poor indeed – a great many are suffering
from measles.

March 25th: Attendance very poor indeed all week. Highest
number present: 199. Miss Carryer is still away
and as the attendance is so very poor think it
advisable to work all the classes in one school.

June 7th: School reopened yesterday morning. Mistress
absent. Miss Carryer resumed her duties and
Louisa Kirby has commenced as a monitor.

June 10th: A great many children attend very irregularly.
Gave school attendance visitor a list of these
children yesterday. Maud Winfield has neglected
her lessons frequently. I spoke to her sharply on
the subject and she promised to be more careful.

June 17th: School closed this afternoon until Monday,
June 27th – the buildings being required next
week for the jubilee celebrations. The children
have been very restless and fidgety all week,
owing no doubt to the heat, and there are many
attending very irregularly.

June 27th: School reopened this morning. Attendance good.
Harriet Wills is suffering with bad eyes and
unable to be at school.

June 30th: Have examined the first four classes this week.
The first two did creditably in all subjects.
The children in the Class Three make very little
progress: the reason being that the majority
of the children in the class attend so badly.

The Class Four did poor work. As a rule they do their work well so the results this week may be attributable to the exam being given directly after the holiday. Maud Winfield has again given me trouble with regard to her lessons.

July 8th: Harriet Wills is still absent. Heard the pupil teachers give object lessons during the week and observed an improvement.

August 18th: School closed today for the usual Fair Holiday, to be reopened on Monday, September 5th.

September 5th: School reopened this morning. Attendance good. The pupil teachers will receive their lessons from seven o'clock until eight each morning, instead of from twelve noon till one.

September 16th: Miss Everitt has been away from school since Tuesday owing to illness. The timetable has not been strictly kept the last few days as a monitress has had to take Miss Everitt's class. Gave pupil teachers an examination last Saturday. Papers pretty well done except Maud Winfield's arithmetic paper, which showed signs of carelessness.

September 23rd: Alma Winfield has been absent from school all week, owing to illness. Miss Everitt is back again. Attendance during the week has been very good, but yesterday afternoon a great many children stayed away – the Statutes being held in the town.

Mr Chawner came to school yesterday to enquire about a child whose finger got hurt in school, as the mother had applied to the Board for recompense. Children have learnt two new songs this week.

September 30th: Alma Winfield has been away from school this week and all of last week. Have examined the classes in the upper division this week.

The children were very restless and fidgety during the exam; consequently the work was not well done. The order is not satisfactory especially in Classes One and Two. The pupil teachers' exam papers were carefully done last week. Maud Winfield is still very careless over her arithmetic.

October 7th: Miss Wells was obliged to leave school early yesterday morning on account of illness and has been away today as well. One of the pupil teachers had to take the little ones during her absence. There has been an improvement in the order this week. Points which pointed out at exam have been attended to. Alma Winfield is back at school, but does not seem well and is very spiritless about her work. She has not been able to come to lessons at seven o'clock with the other teachers.

October 15th: Several children admitted this morning, and one or two back at school who have been absent some time suffering from scarlatina. Pupil teachers' examination took place Saturday last.

October 17th: Revd HMI. Capel signed new timetables from which we shall now work.

October 28th: Have examined the classes in the senior department this week and was pleased with the improvement in each class. The order was much better and the children answered better. Arithmetic is the worst subject in all the classes. The children in the Class Three attend badly and are consequently very backward indeed. Louisa Kirby absent Wednesday and Thursday on account of sickness.

November 27th: School closed this afternoon owing to Sanger's Circus being in the town. Florence Lees absent on account of illness.

Cavendish Council Infants, Standard 1.

December 9th: Attendance very poor, especially in the junior department, owing to sickness and severity of the weather. Since Maud Winfield was transferred, Alma has taken her class and gives satisfaction. Laura Kirby is also a promising teacher. Grace Wells has improved very much lately in her manner of conducting gallery lessons and in teaching singing.

Miss Everitt has taught a new song this week viz. 'The Sparrow on the Tree'.

1888

February 24th: On Monday last, sixty-three girls were transferred to the girls' department and fifty-six boys to the boys' department.

March 2nd: The classes have been arranged as follows:

Class One Div. (a)	Alma Winfield	Pupil Teacher
Class One Div. (b)	Miss Wells	Assistant
Class Two Div. (a)	Louisa Kirby & H. Wills	Monitors
Class Two Div. (b)	Florence Lees	Pupil Teacher

Miss G. Wells will take the babies' class and Miss Carryer will take the management of the junior department.

April 9th: Took charge of this school today (signed) A. Godfrey, Class Two Certificated Teacher.

April 20th: Have examined the classes this week and find they are making fair progress in their work. The arithmetic is the worst subject.

April 27th: Gave a list of absentees to the attendance visitor today. Many children absent this week owing to the stormy weather.

May 1st: Miss G. Wells has been transferred to the girls' department. Florence Lees will take her place in the babies' room and Harriet Wills will take the Class One in the junior department.

Harriet Townsend commenced duties today as a monitress: age on May 5th 1875, thirteen years old.

Certificate awarded to William Knight by the Inkberrow School Board, Worcestershire, on passing the First Standard on May 1st 1888. Similar certificates were awarded by schools across Leicestershire.

May 9th: Heard teachers give object lessons. Alma Winfield did not make hers as interesting as she might have done; consequently, the order was not what it should have been. I have pointed out mistakes to her. Harriet Wills' lesson was given much better in every respect than last week. The children answered more carefully and there was an improvement in the order of the class.

May 18th: School closed for the usual Whitsuntide Holiday.

June 2nd: The attendance has been good through the week but there are still some who attend irregularly and some are absent with whooping cough. Average attendance: 316. Highest number: 328.

June 8th: Teachers have not kept their classes in very good order this week. Children have been especially noisy during gallery lessons; have spoken to teachers about it.

June 13th: Three boys came too late for their attendance mark.

June 18th: Have admitted a girl seven years of age. She has never been to school before so is not fit for the girls' school.

June 29th: Have heard teachers' object lessons during the week and discern an improvement in each. Alma Winfield does her work in a noisy manner and find her class working in the same way; have spoken to her about it.

July 2nd: Florence Toft commences duties as monitress today.

July 27th: Have examined the classes this week. The Class One have done better work this month. Reading is still the worst subject. The Class Two have not made such improvement as I should like, probably owing to the irregular attendance

of the scholars. Have pointed out defects to the
teachers and hope for an improvement.

August 2nd: School closed yesterday on account of the Church
School Treat. Attendance has been good throughout
the week. Average: 350. Highest present: 365.

August 7th: School closed yesterday, it being Bank Holiday.

August 17th: School closed today for the usual Fair Holiday,
to be reopened September 10th.

September 14th: The order throughout the school has been good
this week and the teachers have worked well with
their classes. Miss Wells taught the children a new
song viz. 'The Soldier Boy'.

September 21st: During the week I have examined the scholars in
the senior department. The Class One did their
work very fairly. Reading is still behind the other
work. The Class Two did not do so well, which
seems to discourage the teacher. Most of the
children are slow and backward.

October 4th: Have examined the Class One in the Junior
School. They have improved considerably but are
still backward. Reading was the best subject.

October 26th: Took charge of the Infants' School on Monday,
October 22nd (signed) M.A. Powers.
    Florence Lees was taken ill in the examination
room on Saturday and not able to go on with her
work. A doctor's certificate was filed with her
papers to that effect. Has been absent all the week.
Alma Winfield has also been away. The following
certificate was handed to me on Wednesday:

'This is to certify that Miss Alma Winfield is ill and not
able to follow her employment.' (signed) Dr Pritchard.

Applied to the Board on Thursday for a teacher to take her place and am authorised to get one.

November 2nd: Began to take the teachers for lessons from eight o'clock to nine. Punished several children for arriving late.

November 9th: Attendance poor on Friday owing to the bad weather. Punished John Ellis and Fred Pinchess on Wednesday afternoon for playing truant, they had both been absent a week.

Having been unsuccessful in obtaining a teacher, applied to the Board for an Assistant Mistress and they have decided to advertise for one.

November 16th: Gave a list of irregular attendees to attendance officer. Punished P. Bailey, C. Smith and F. Mustin for playing truant.

November 23rd: Florence Lees, who has been absent from lessons since the examination, began to come again on Monday. Miss Hames absent on Thursday and Friday ill. Have taken the Class One this week as we are still short of a teacher. Miss Wells has taken the second and third division of Class One with the help of Rose Jackson, who commenced as monitress here on Monday.

November 30th: Mr Heaton complained of the behaviour of the teachers at drawing on Saturday morning. Gave them a good talking to and found that it was through some nonsense on the part of Rose Jackson.

Punished John Ellis, at his father's request, on Monday afternoon for playing truant.

December 7th: Miss M. Taunt appointed Assistant Mistress.

Had to complain to Ruth Jackson for throwing water over, as Harriet Townsend was bringing it across the playground for the children to wash in.

December 14th: Mrs Brown came to school on Wednesday afternoon and was very abusive to Miss Carryer for slapping her Lizzie. The child attends very badly and is inattentive when she is here. It seems in the morning that Miss Carryer gave her a slap and Mr Burton had also visited the woman, so she thought she had just cause of complaint.

December 21st: Examined the whole school. Progress satisfactory. Writing in the Class Two wants attention. Sent home several children for their school money. Closed school on Thursday afternoon for Christmas Holiday.

Awarded to Harry Lualington when inspected by HMI J.R. Blakiston on July 10th 1888 to certify he had passed Standard Four. This example is from Barrow School, Wentworth.

Four

a New Book, *1889–1893*

The entry dated April 19th 1889 closes the school's first logbook. Despite financial difficulties and problems with health and social conditions, the introduction of a School Savings Scheme is well supported.

1889

January 4th: Opened school on Monday morning after a week's holiday with 288 present and the attendance did not improve much all week.

Harry Farmer tumbled in the playground on Friday morning and bumped his head very badly. I bathed it well and then sent one of the teachers home with him.

January 11th: Sent W. Crofts home for his school money as his father was in work and he brought no excuse. Received rather an insulting note from the father saying he hadn't one to send.

Attended the audit at the workhouse on Friday morning and again on Saturday.

January 18th: Miss Wells taught a new song 'Now We Little Children'. Have been working from the new timetables this week, as by the old ones no class had more than one hour a week appointed for number, and the four-year-old class only half hour. Attendance better, especially in the junior department.

January 25th: Gave a list to attendance officer of all children who have been absent for the last three weeks. In most cases illness was assigned to the cause.

February 1st: Sent George Blower and Sam Pratt home until they should be better, as they had ringworm.

February 8th: Sent George Paul home as he was suffering from blister pox.

February 15th: A wretched attendance on Monday morning owing to the snow, only 129 present. Worked all in the junior department. Miss Hames taken ill again in school on Monday afternoon and has not been able to attend since.

February 22nd: Miss Hames still absent and likely to be for some time. Miss B. Pickering came on Monday to take the class until after the examination. Sent after irregular attendees. Punished T.A. Clarke and M. Bolton for coming late and losing their attendance.

March 1st: School examined by Revd Capel, HM Inspector on Monday, Tuesday and Wednesday.
    Mrs Bailey came to complain of Lizzie's jacket being torn and the buttons cut off. Warned children against touching other children's clothes.
    Gave out certificates on Thursday afternoon to those children who attended the last twenty-two weeks of the school year.

March 8th: Drafted the Class One from the junior department to the senior. Lily Orton and Harriet Townsend have taken the new Class One this week and have managed them well. Gave each teacher a list of object lessons for her class for 1889.

A half-holiday was given on Tuesday
(Shrove Tuesday).

March 15th: Miss G. Wells came to school on Monday morning
to say her sister Miss E. Wells had gone out for a
few days. Mr Kiddle at night informed me that she
had severed her connection with the school.

Sent note to Mr Chawner on Tuesday
morning asking him to visit the school which he
did and gave permission that Miss Pickering be
asked to come to help until further arrangements
could be made. She came in the afternoon.

Messrs Pilgrim, Hall and Goode visited on
Thursday morning at twelve o'clock and went through
the list of school requisites that I laid before them and
the need of two assistants being engaged; one in the
place of Miss Wells and the other for Standard One.

At the meeting on Thursday night, Miss Wells
asked to be re-engaged and to begin duties again
on March 25th: was granted on conditions. Clerk
instructed to advertise for one Assistant Mistress
as soon as possible.

Drafted forty boys to the boys' department and
forty girls to the girls' department, also two classes of
four-year-olds from the junior department to senior.
Harriet Wills and Lily Orton came up with these
classes, and have transferred Harriet Townsend and
Miss Hames to the junior department.

March 22nd: Miss Hames came in school on Monday
afternoon and began her duties again on Tuesday.
Florence Lees has taken the Class One girls this
week. Lily Orton taken ill in school on Tuesday
morning and had to send her home for the rest of
the day, also absent by permission from lessons on
Wednesday and Thursday.

Harriet Wills gave a good lesson on 'The Camel'
and kept good order. Have taken all the classes in
turn this week.

March 29th: Miss Wells returned to school on Monday morning. Miss Pickering was appointed Assistant Mistress on Thursday, to commence duties on April 1st.

April 5th: Gave a fresh supply of reading books, slates and pencils to each teacher.

    Have arranged that Miss Wells shall take the singing this year, Miss Taunt drill and Miss Hames recitation in the junior department. Each teacher to take her own class for tonic sol-fa.

April 12th: Gave a model lesson on 'a chair' to Class Four. Began to teach a new kindergarten game: The Mill. Teachers have worked well this week.

    Sent William Hawkins home on Friday morning with bad ears and told him he had better not come again until they were better.

April 19th: Harriet Townsend absent the whole week with a bad cold, and Harriet Wills on Tuesday with face-ache. Received the Report on 17th April and Mr Kiddle entered it the same afternoon in the new logbook. Closed school on Thursday morning for the Easter Holidays.

Pages from the Hinckley Board School logbook showing the Report of the Annual Examination by Her Majesty's Inspector dated April 17th 1889.

May 3rd: Attendance pretty good on Monday after the
Easter Holidays. John Thorn played truant on
Monday and Tuesday and spent his school money.
Ada Needham and Margaret Harrold commenced
work as monitors.

May 10th: Lily Orton's indentures signed. Sent Thomas
Burton and Robert Groves home with blister pox.

May 17th: Had the gallery marked for drill. Charles Smith
a boy in the Class One was run over on Tuesday
and had his leg broken in two places. Punished
William Hewins, Fred Puffer, William White and
Arthur Dorman for playing truant. Warned Lily
Orton and the teachers generally against boxing
the children's ears.

May 31st: Punished Tom Dale for playing truant and
spending his school money, at his mother's request.
Spoke to Miss Carryer about being severe with the
babies and asked her to let them play more.

June 21st: Sent Walter and Ada Brown, Dinah and Arthur
Dorman and Ian Pratt home on Friday with sores
on their hands until they shall be better. Maud
Faulkeney has gone into the workhouse with an
infectious skin disease.

June 28th: Mrs Dorman sent her children to school again
on Monday but I sent them home again. Louisa
Farmer and Sophia Briggs both away with the
same disease, itch. Have also sent Ada Dixon and
Paul home on suspicion. Attendance fallen off very
much the last few days owing to the erroneous
report that the itch is very common amongst the
children and the parents thinking that they are safer
at home. Many women came to school on Friday
to enquire into it and went away quite satisfied and
sent their children to school at once.

July 5th: Attendance a little better but still a lot away through fear of infection. Attendance officer visited most of these and explained that there was no reason whatever to keep the children at home. Sent Lizzie Hicken home with a breakout on her hands and arms on Thursday. Mother came up for an explanation and promised to keep her away until quite well.

July 19th: Mrs Bailey came to school on Friday morning and asked me to lock Percy and Albert in at dinnertime to see if it would cure them of playing truant. They have run away five times this week.

July 26th: Mrs Brown came to school on Wednesday to complain of Miss Pickering caning and marking her child. I went thoroughly into the case while the mother was here and found nothing of the sort had taken place, but that the boy had been fighting after school.

August 2nd: Percy and Albert Bailey locked in school on Wednesday and Friday all dinnertime for playing truant (at the mother's request who brought them something to eat).

September 13th: Opened school on Monday morning with a good attendance. Admitted sixteen new children. Several children away with measles. One child died during the holiday and three have left the town.

October 11th: Edith Knight died of typhoid fever. Measles on the increase. Punished Albert Bailey for playing truant and spending his school money.

November 22nd: Wrote a note to the Board suggesting that a piano be bought for the senior department and the harmonium be transferred to the junior.

Detail from the Hinckley Board School logbook dated
October 11th 1889.

November 29th: Punished Ada and Alfred Warren for playing
truant. May Hamson and Arthur Dorman left in
the classroom by mistake on Friday dinnertime
until half past one by Harriet Wells; sent her to
the mother to explain. They were quite satisfied.

December 20th: Have examined all the classes with satisfactory
results. School fees badly paid, the excuse brought
'father has no work' in nearly all cases. School closed
today (Thursday) for the Christmas Holidays.

1890

January 3rd: School opened after the Christmas Holidays. Sent
Joseph C. home on Monday morning to be made
clean; he was filthy and not fit to be against anyone.

January 24th: Punished John Palmer for picking Nathan Toone's
pocket and taking a half-penny, which he spent.
Complained to Lily Orton about the careless way she
deals with her class; also to all of the teachers about
the needless noise made in changing the lessons.

Examined all the school. Have taken the dunces
out of the Standard One and put them in another
class, it being impossible to do anything with
them in that class.

February 7th: Sent Agnes Bloxham and Lizzie Mansfield home on Thursday afternoon, both having sores on their heads, and told them to stay away until they were better.

February 28th: Messrs Taylor, Bott and Buckingham (Visiting Committee) came into school on Tuesday morning. Asked them to give prizes to the regular attenders instead of certificates as has been the custom.

March 7th: Received the prizes for the children who attended 400 times or more during the last school year.

April 4th: Punished Sarah Dixon and Frank Bloxham for spending school money and playing truant.

June 13th: Mrs Bailey found Albert playing truant on Wednesday morning and brought him to school giving him a good thrashing in the cap room with a stick she brought with her.

    Had ten children come in after the registers were closed on Friday afternoon: sent them all home again, hoping it would be more of a punishment than keeping them, as some of them have habitually come in late.

July 18th: School attendance officer visited and reported on the absentees; gave him a new list. Mrs Pratt came to school very indignant at her boy William being sent home to ask for his school money. She threatened to keep him at home for the rest of the week, which she did.

August 1st: Punished Katie Turner for spending her school money.

September 12th: Opened school on Monday with a good attendance: 398 present. Refused admission to children under three as the baby room is full. Admitted Beatrice Wallace, a girl over seven who has no idea of her letters; have put her in a class accordingly.

An unknown Victorian class.

October 10th: Sent notes to parents who are in arrears for school fees. Very few sent it.

October 17th: Complained to Lily Orton of the noisy and rough way she deals with her class and told her unless she alters I shall be obliged to take her class away and give it to another teacher. A little improvement in roughness but very little quieter.

October 31st: Took the children for dumb-bell drill instead of kindergarten.

November 7th: Had to be very cross with Lily Orton and Florence Toft for neglect of their work and general idleness on Wednesday morning. Attendance very bad the whole of Friday owing to the stormy weather.

November 21st: Gave a model lesson in paper folding to the Class Two on Monday afternoon. Examined the junior department: progress satisfactory.

Warned Florence Toft about the danger of boxing ears, which she is very apt to do.

December 19th: The Visiting Committee came in on Thursday morning; asked them about having the lines repainted for drill and that the gas burners might be attended to.

1891

January 23rd: The junior large room and one classroom were
                       used on Thursday afternoon for an ambulance
                       examination, at which Miss Heath, Miss Gaunt
                       and myself attended.

February 20th: Had to speak very strongly to Lily Orton and
                       Florence Toft about their bad behaviour at the draw-
                       ing class, and their general conduct out of school.

March 13th: Lizzie Foxon lost her jacket last week out of the
                       porch and we have failed, so far, to find it. The mother
                       has informed me she shall not pay school money for
                       any of her children until she gets it back.
                           Report received 1st April 1891:

                       The infants are in good order and generally well taught.

April 17th: Mrs Stevens came to school on Thursday to say
                       that Alfred had been playing truant all the week,
                       and asked me to punish him when he returned.
                       Talked to him on Friday and on him promising
                       not to do it again forgave him.

April 24th: Alfred Stevens played truant on Friday afternoon
                       last week and three times thus: punished him as
                       requested by his mother.

May 15th: Attendance poor and fees badly paid, owing to the
                       parents being out of work through the strike.

June 5th: The Traveller from the Midland Educational
                       Company came in on Tuesday afternoon. Sent in
                       a list of school requisites to the Board.

July 10th: Sent for Willie Hickens' mother on Thursday
                       morning as I found he was peeling after

scarlet fever. He was away a fortnight ago for
some days with toothache it was said, but now
find that he had a rash. Had the school sprinkled
well with disinfectant and wrote to the Medical
Officer informing him of the case.

July 31st: Three children absent with whooping cough and
many with feverish colds.

August 7th: Lizzie Collier took a piece of knitting out of school
on Thursday afternoon and also picked a girl's pocket
of a farthing, which she spent. Was afraid to punish
her except by making her sit by herself as she has sore
eyes and seems altogether in a weakly state.

September 11th: Opened school on Monday morning after three
weeks holiday with a very good attendance: 439
present. Had to send home several children suffering from whooping cough, which seems to be on
the increase.

  No fees collected. Board decided to make this a
free school.

September 18th: A holiday given on Thursday afternoon owing to
the Statutes for the hiring of servants being held.

October 30th: Mrs Colver summoned for the irregular
attendance of Louise. After the Magistrates'
meeting on Monday, she came to school and was
very abusive, laying down the law very strongly
how her children were to be taught &c.

November 6th: Punished Albert Payne, Bertie and Harry
Wheat and Frank Bloxham for playing truant.
Mr Charner visited on Wednesday morning
and I asked him to speak to Payne, who is the
ringleader in all this running away. He did so and
also suggested a notice being sent to his parents to
attend the Board meeting, which was done.

November 27th: Received a new scale of salaries for assistants.

SCALE OF TEACHER SALARIES

		MALES			FEMALES		
Candidates	(13 years of age)	10	0	0	8	0	0
Pupil Teachers	1st year	13	10	0	11	10	0
"	2nd year	17	0	0	15	0	0
"	3rd year	20	10	0	18	10	0
"	4th year	24	0	0	22	0	0
Assistants (Ex. P.T.)	1st year	45	0	0	35	0	0
" "	2nd year	50	0	0	40	0	0
Certificated "	1st year	55	0	0	45	0	0
" "	2nd year	60	0	0	50	0	0
On receiving Parchment...		65	0	0	55	0	0

Scale of teacher salaries for 1891. An annual increase of
salary was at the discretion of the Board, having regard to
the Report of the Annual Examination.

December 4th: Attendance fallen off again owing to children
having bad coughs and colds and some blister
pox. Punished Ernest Smith for playing truant.
Received seventeen new dual desks.

December 18th: Messrs Bott and Taylor visited on Wednesday
morning to discuss the question of the new scale
of salaries. The assistants are dissatisfied because
the assistants in the girls' school are to have
£2 10s a year more than the infants'. They have
written to the Board asking them to reconsider
the question and make the salaries equal for the
same qualification.

December 25th: Assistants received notice during the week from
the Board that they might be paid by the old scale
or the new, whichever they preferred.

1892

January 8th: Opened school on Monday morning. Commenced taking money for the Savings Bank, according to instructions received from the Board. At nine o'clock, eighty-six children had entered.

January 15th: Had to send John W. home as he was not in a fit state to be in a class. The mother came and explained the reason. Attendance officer promised to bring the matter before the Board and report.

March 11th: School Attendance Committee, Mr Bott and Mr Taylor, came on Thursday morning and went through the list of requisites. Asked for curtains to divide the classes in the junior department.

April 8th: John W. returned to school after a long absence. Have decided that he would be better in the Infants' School for another year as he is subject to fits and general weakness.

May 27th: Admitted a girl, Miriam Higginson aged six years, last March. She has not the slightest idea of writing and cannot tell one letter from another.

July 1st: Wrote to the Board asking them for two more teachers as the classes are too large for good work to be done.

July 15th: Mrs Gilder came in Friday afternoon to complain of Miss Gaunt punishing her boy and to say she would not have him hit. Spoke to Miss Gaunt about it and found he had been very disobedient in the morning and she smacked him.

September 9th: Opened school after three weeks holiday with
a fair attendance (434 present). Measles have
spread amongst the children. Two deaths in the
babies' class: Walter Barrett and Prudence Finney.
Have sent home all children where I know they
have measles in the house.

September 16th: Admitted Nellie Armstrong on Monday morning,
but as she upset the whole school was obliged to
send her home. Found she was insane.
        Gave a list of absentees to the visiting officer.
Had five of the blackboards renovated.

September 23rd: Mrs Arguile came on Wednesday morning to
complain of Miss Gent caning Nellie. Upon inves-
tigation I found that during the playtime the said
teacher had a pointer in her hand and accidentally
scratched her neck as she was moving around.
        A holiday given on Thursday afternoon on account
of the Statutes for the hiring of servants being held.

November 11th: Attendance fallen off again. Harriet Wills
visited most absentees and found no fresh cases
of measles, but children suffering with coughs.
Florence Toft still absent by order of the doctor.
She is suffering from weakness.

Children's desks were equipped with inkwells for dipping
pens. This example was manufactured by William Fisher
& Son from West Bromwich. (Photo by permission of
Chilvers Coton Heritage Centre)

Spoke very sharply to Lily Orton on
Wednesday morning for ill manners and sulkiness.
She has behaved better since.

November 25th: Received notice from the Board that all children
suffering with bad heads were to be sent home
at once and a note with them telling the parents
the reason.

1893

January 20th: Lily Orton very snappy and cross with her
children. When I spoke to her received the answer
she was put out about several things.

February 24th: Mr Bott and Mr Taylor, Visiting Committee,
came in on Tuesday afternoon. Gave permission
to me to buy toys as usual for the children who
attended 400 times and over during the past year.

March 3rd: Mr Hugill came to see me on Thursday to say
he wished Violet to take First Year's Papers next
October. He said he had studied 'The Code' and
found the work nothing to a clever girl like Violet
and he was confident she would come out Class One.
I told him my opinion was quite different. I found
her backward instead of brilliant, and to her the work
would be very hard, if not an impossibility in the
time. I promised to speak to the Visiting Committee
about it, but I thought in the interest of the girl she
should not be presented as a pupil teacher this year.

March 10th: Mr Griffiths, Mr Taylor, Mr Bott and Mr Smith
visited on Tuesday morning. I laid the wish of
Mr Hugill respecting his daughter before them.
It was decided to comply with it, on the
understanding that if things went contrary to his
expectations, no blame should be attached to me.

April 21st: The Board request the logbook to be on the Board table at every meeting.

Report received 29th April 1893 (boys' department):

The discipline is good, and so with rather less general noise, would be the order. The work is fairly well done as regards both accuracy and intelligence.

May 12th: George Wilson picked up a shilling in school on Monday morning, and spent 7*d* and gave 5*d* to his father. Made enquiries but failed to find who had lost it. Mr Burton went to see Mr Wilson who refused to return it until the owner was found.

May 19th: Mrs Mason came to school on Monday to say she sent a shilling the week before to be put into Arthur's book, but she found it hadn't been entered, and he said he dropped it in school. Sent Mr Burton to tell Mr Wilson and he returned it.

May 29th: The following is a copy of resolution passed at the Board Meeting: 'That in future the monitors and Pupil Teachers receive instruction at least ten hours per week. For the winter months of the year not to meet for lessons before 8 a.m. Mr Heaton to have charge of the Boys and Miss Teal the Girls in her Department, Miss Powers to have charge of all Pupil Teachers in the Infant Dept. Saturday morning from 9 to 12 and one evening from 6.30 to 8.30.'

June 2nd: Walter Puffer died of scarlatina.

A policeman came to school on Thursday afternoon to enquire for George Moore, Gus Whitmore, Charles Blower and Fred Payne, who had been taking gooseberries from Mrs Lord's orchard. He took their ages and told them they would hear from him again.

June 13th: Walter Chamberlain at school this morning.
                    Has been away since May 30th. Had scarlatina.
                    His hands were 'all peeling'. Sent him home at once.

June 22nd: George Garratt at school again this afternoon. Sent
                    him home on Monday because his hands were
                    peeling. Sent him away again as his hands were only
                    half peeled; the skin coming off in large patches. Any
                    wonder that scarlatina spreads from one to another.

July 7th: School closed on Wednesday afternoon for the
                    rest of the week on account of the Royal Wedding.
                    Had to speak to F. Toft about keeping her class in
                    and then leaving them to take care of themselves
                    while she went into a classroom to gossip.

August 4th: Copy books of Class Three were very
                    disappointing – called teachers' attention to same.

September 15th: Violet Hugill not at school on Monday. Sent to
                    ask where she was and received the following
                    reply, 'The Board knows and so does Mr Heaton.'

September 20th: The following boys have gone to the Grammar
                    School having gained free scholarships: Tom C.
                    Reynolds, Fred Reppen and George Goadby.

September 21st: Notice brought of the death of William Baker a
                    boy in the Class Five from 'Typhoid Fever'.

September 22nd: Mrs Sharpe came to school in a great rage on
                    Tuesday morning about eleven o'clock saying
                    Walter had run home at playtime and told
                    her how Miss Gent had been thrashing him.
                    Miss Gent denied having touched him but said
                    she had told him to stop in after twelve o'clock
                    for idleness. The mother wouldn't believe her and
                    was most abusive both in manner and speech.
                    At last I persuaded her to fetch the boy when it

was found he had made up a tale because he didn't want to stop at school. Mrs Sharpe gave him a thrashing for telling lies and apologised most humbly to Miss Gent for her unjust treatment.

September 28th: Gave lesson to Class Five on 'Numeration'. Tried to impress upon the children's minds the necessity of putting figures down carefully and arranging sums tidily on their slates. Showed them the difference between a slate with work put down carelessly and another one where scholar has tried to show off his work to best advantage.

Had to speak to Miss Herbert about striking the children in her class.

October 21st: Found a child shut up in the lavatory of the junior department on Wednesday afternoon. Upon enquiry found that Clara Robottom put her there because she was naughty. Commanded her never to do such a thing again.

October 28th: Sent home (after advice from the Medical Officer of Health) all children that I knew had anyone at home with a bad throat.

Sarah and Ethel Ball died of diphtheria.

November 4th: Sent several children home with bad throats.

Alice Dix died of diphtheria.

November 11th: Attendance not as good this week. Sore throats and bad colds prevalent.

Nellie Holland went into the junior department on Wednesday morning at twelve o'clock over a child's jacket and used very bad language to the teachers. A policeman had to be called to send her away as she would not go for any one of them.

Agnes Collins died of diphtheria.

November 18th: Joseph Dix died of diphtheria.

November 23rd: The following is a copy of certificate given this morning: 'Jos T. Bray has attended the Hinckley Board Schools 28 times out of a possible 106 since September 11th. He was last in school on October 12th.'

November 25th: Cautioned May Reynolds against boxing children.

November 29th: Schools visited this morning by S.W. Wheaton Inspector from Local Government Board with regard to the prevalence of diphtheria in Hinckley and District. Here from ten o'clock till quarter to twelve. Nine suspicious cases of sore throat were picked out. I sent them home at once with a note stating the reason.

December 2nd: Elsie and Ethel Wykes, Beatrice Spoard and Harold Gregory died of diphtheria.

December 4th: Harry Simmons in Class Two returned to school this morning. Last attendance made September 19th. Not one of the brightest of children at best. Am afraid that he will have to be put in Class Three as the work of Class Two is far away ahead of him. Shall try him this week.

December 8th: The following is a copy of letter received from Local Sanitary Authority by Mr T. Kiddle, Clerk, School Board: 'I am directed by the Hinckley Local Board to give you notice and require you to close the Hinckley Board Schools for a period of six weeks from the date of receipt of this letter for the purpose of preventing the spread of the epidemic of diphtheria in the town. The Board are acting upon the advice of their Medical Officer.

I beg to refer you to Article 88 of the New Code of Regulations issued by the Education Department in 1893 giving the Sanitary Authority power to close Elementary Schools to prevent the spread of disease.'

Five

Diphtheria, 1894–1896

The year 1894 begins late, the school having been closed by order of the Medical Authority in an effort to halt the spread of diphtheria. Conditions in the classroom improve slightly when the head teacher has cause to intervene and complain about the violent behaviour of the teachers!

1894

January 26th: Schools reopened on Thursday morning, January 25th, having been closed since December 8th by Medical Authority on account of the epidemic of diphtheria. All the classrooms cleaned and disinfected. In place of closure, we could well have done with two or three weeks extra schooling. The constant absence of children from personal or sickness at home is showing itself materially in the progress of many children.

January 31st: Joseph Mitchell gave a geography lesson. A more frequent use of chalk and blackboard would be a great advantage to both scholars and teacher.

February 2nd: Attendance very fair. Many children who have been away a long time have returned.

So far have lost twenty-two children from this department with diphtheria: four boys and eighteen girls.

February 16th: Second year pupil teachers had their bi-monthly examination on Saturday. Violet Hugill failed in history and geography.

March 15th: Crofts, a boy in the Class Five, away this morning. Locked him in school on Tuesday and Wednesday during the dinner hour at the request of his father, for playing truant. The punishment does not seem on the face of it to have been effective.

April 20th: Mr Taylor visited on Thursday morning and Mr Goode and Mr Bott in the afternoon: brought before them V. Hugill's inability to teach and the unsatisfactoriness of her lessons.

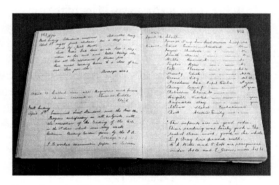

Pages from the Hinckley Board School logbook dated April 1894.

April 27th: Readmitted Ed Kirchin and Ernest Maypole during the week, as also a younger brother of the latter. Left us about twelve months ago, presumably they have been attending the Catholic School, although in reality one would imagine they had been about the streets if one has to judge of their attainments.

May 4th: Found several boys have been playing truant lately.
They have not yet got into the usual groove of
attending school. Have sent after several. Others
have had to bring a book with them so as to have
the daily attendance put in.

Took V. Hugill to task on Wednesday afternoon
for saying I didn't give her a chance to teach and
told her she was telling falsehoods and that she
ought to tell her father so. I recalled to her mind
classes I had tried her with, the teachers after school
testifying to this. Gave her a class at once and told
her for the future I should expect her to do the
work. On Thursday morning I received a note from
Mr Hugill saying my 'uncalled for language' had
upset Violet and she would not be at school that day.

May 21st: Reopened school today. The smallness in the attendance may be accounted for in the cases of smallpox
in the town. Many of the parents are keeping their
children away as a safeguard – keep the various parts
of the building liberally sprinkled with disinfectant.

May 31st: The following is a copy of the return for the department showing number of boys who have left the
Upper Standards in the year ending May 31st 1894,
to follow the under mentioned occupations:

Hosiery Factory	3
Carpenter	2
Needle making	5
Baker	1
Errand Boys	2
Office Boy	1
Farm Boy	1
Left the Town	3
Grammar School	9
Transferred to Half-Time Department	24

June 1st: Attendance very poor all week. Many parents keeping their children away because of the smallpox; four or five are suffering with it, and about a dozen families have it in the home and children have either been kept or sent away from school in consequence.

June 15th: Find that both diphtheria and scarlet fever are present again in the town and had two or three cases reported. This, with the smallpox epidemic, is making sad havoc not with attendance only, but with the progress of the scholars, as I found on examining Classes Three and Four in dictation and spelling.

June 21st: Miss Herbert complained about the boy Moore, who was admitted on Monday. He appears to have been running the streets for some time. It would seem as if it had been a long time for the boy does not appear to know his letters.

June 22nd: James S. died of diphtheria and Walter Flude of bronchitis.

V. Hugill manages the few children I give her with so little success that I have arranged for her to help Miss Taylor for some time.

July 5th: Joseph Bray and Kirchin went off at playtime. Cancelled their attendances. The former has made eight attendances since Whit week and today is his first appearance for this week.

Mrs Robinson brought a medical certificate for her son Thomas suffering from debility. Has been nine times since April 13th.

July 6th: Heard today of the death of A. Clark (Class Four) from diphtheria.

July 13th: Mrs G. sent Percy again on Monday morning, though I had distinctly told her she must keep him away a fortnight. Sent him back. Also sent

Matthew Johnson home for another week, as his
mother was removed to the smallpox hospital a
week ago.

Gave a list of absentees of children over five
years to Mr Burton and Miss Wills and I visited
all under. Found six or seven away on account
of diphtheria, five with blister pox – a few been
vaccinated and the rest away with bad colds &c.

The Board has decided that when any teacher
wants to be absent, the head is to refer them
to the Chairman. In no case is a teacher to
be absent through illness without sending a
medical note.

July 24th: Mrs Hydon called in the afternoon respecting her
boy Thomas. Had him at the Cottage Hospital.
The boy is right below the mark and, lately,
complained about not being able to see to read
or write.

July 25th: Mrs Crofts came about her son, George, who was
taken yesterday to the Birmingham Eye Hospital.
Brought a medical certificate stating that the boy
is not in a condition for any indoor work and
ought not to attend school.

August 10th: Violet Hugill's lessons prepared badly all the week.

September 21st: Attendance fallen off a little. Four or five cases of
diphtheria reported.

September 28th: A holiday given on Thursday afternoon owing to a
circus visiting the town.
        Nellie Pratt died of diphtheria.

October 5th: Got Mr Perkins to play on the harmonium a
marching tune whilst the boys were entering and
leaving the room. The hollow floor helps largely to
contribute to the noise whilst this is being done.

One is apt to think enviously of those who have central halls and solid block floors.

Lily Orton and Ada Needham received notice on Thursday morning that they had passed the Scholarship Examination.

October 26th: Took Class Seven for writing – some good examples. One boy (Simmons) did not do his writing, gave the excuse that he was not able to see his work. This is one of the after-effects of diphtheria.

Lily Smith died of diphtheria and many more cases reported.

November 2nd: Harry Calvert and Lilian Bedford died of diphtheria.

November 9th: Five fresh cases of diphtheria reported, and one death, Kate Flude. Several children suffering with blister pox.

November 16th: Mr Burton reported twelve fresh cases of diphtheria of children attending this school. One death, Nellie Maw.

November 20th: Readmitted William Alsopp this morning. By the admission register he was ten last February. Been away from here since November 10th 1892. His time has been spent in the streets.

November 23rd: Horace Wain and Priscilla Payne died of diphtheria.

November 30th: Several children returned after diphtheria. Herbert Hamson died on Thursday; was in school the Friday before.

Miss Mawby died on Wednesday of consumption. Had been away from school since May 29th.

The teacher's desk was placed at the front of the classroom facing the children. (Photo by permission of Chilvers Coton Heritage Centre)

December 21st: Several fresh cases of diphtheria reported and two of blister pox.

1895

January 4th: Schools thoroughly disinfected during the holidays.

January 7th: Heard that Thomas Robinson, a boy in
Class Seven, is dead from diphtheria.
     Told Ridgway brothers to stay at home as there
is a case of diphtheria in the family.

January 18th: Seven or eight cases of whooping cough reported.

February 15th: Mr Burton reported nine fresh cases of diphtheria
and several of whooping cough.

March 7th: Heard today of the death of F. Wykes from
diphtheria. Last at school on February 14th.

March 8th: William Brown died of diphtheria and Alfred had
been attending school all the time. Sent him home
at once and Mr Burton went to caution the mother.

March 11th: Fred Thompson returned to school having
been away since February 6th with diphtheria.
Had paralysis of palate, could not speak distinctly
and he complained of not being able to see the
print of the books.

April 3rd: Attendance visitor came in to report diphtheria
cases at three o'clock. Found Walter Farmer,
brother of one of the recent cases at school. Sent
him home at once. He was absent all yesterday
and found on enquiry that it was on account of
the sickness in the family and yet he should be
sent to school today. Some things which are done
are not easily explained.

April 6th: Laura Bray received notice that she had
obtained a Class One Scholarship and that she
might enter Cheltenham Training College on
September 17th next.

April 22nd: Report Received:

The Boys are in good order. Their arithmetic is very well done, but there is a good deal unevenness about the other subjects, both the elementary and additional, which appears to indicate a want of uniformity in the quality of the staff.

The Infants' School is conducted with diligence and vigour, and allowing for much sickness, the work is fairly well done. There appeared however to be some weaknesses about the knowledge of object lessons.

May 3rd: Five fresh cases of diphtheria reported. At the present time as far as known there are only nineteen children in this department absent on account of this disease.

May 10th: Ada Goadby and Uriah Crofts died of diphtheria. Mr Langley, late Staff Sergeant Drill Master, visited the schools and, on Friday morning from ten o'clock to twelve, drilled the children in exercises and figure marching, complimenting them very highly on their marching.

May 24th: Mrs Dawson came to complain of Miss Toft boxing her boy's ears. Has promised to be more careful in future.

June 14th: Allowed children who have attended ten times during the week to take colouring last lesson. This is in place of giving out checks.

June 24th: Readmitted John Sylvester, age eleven, in September. Has been away from school for nearly two years and then previously attended very irregularly on account of illness at home. The attendance visitor tells me he is to attend half-time.

June 28th: The junior department entirely upset from ten o'clock to eleven on Tuesday morning and the whole of Friday afternoon by Walter Butterworth. He had been truanting and on being brought to school rolled on the floor kicking, screaming and tearing his clothes like a mad child, and would not be pacified. At my suggestion his mother stayed on Friday afternoon as she thought he had been punished to make him go into such a passion. She smacked him soundly times and times but it had no effect and at three forty-five in the afternoon she left the school tired out, saying we might do what we liked to him for if she stayed longer she should half kill him.

September 2nd: Reopened school. Readmitted two boys and admitted four others. Amongst the latter is Bertie Wheat, been absent since before examination. Had Saint Vitus Dance.

September 13th: Had colouring again in the afternoon for those boys who have made a full week.

September 27th: Attendance poor, especially on Thursday afternoon when a circus was in the town.

October 4th: Had to warn Miss Toft again about rapping children on their knuckles with a pointer.

October 11th: Received a note from the Board, which I impressed on the teachers, prohibiting the assistants from punishing the children in any way.

October 18th: A holiday given on Monday afternoon owing to a circus being in the town.

October 23rd: Examined Class Six, Standard Two. The after-effects of diphtheria are plainly

evident in this class, quite half of them
being affected.

November 15th: Miss Smith complained of the little use Violet
Hugill is to her, so have arranged that May
Reynolds shall stay in that department this year,
and that V. Hugill shall help Miss Wells.

November 29th: The dull afternoons have been very depressing,
especially as the gas obtained has been hardly
sufficient for one room, so that when distributed
in the boys', girls' and infants' departments it has
not been sufficient to get through the work with
any comfort.

December 6th: Attendance fallen off very much, owing to an
outbreak of measles.

December 13th: Attendance worse and worse. Nearly two-thirds of
the children absent in the junior department.
    Had to complain to May Reynolds for boxing a
boy's ears and behaving roughly to him.

December 20th: A woman came to school on Monday morning
to say May Reynolds had hit her child on the
hand and marked it. On being spoken to about it,
she behaved very insolently and in the afternoon
brought a very threatening letter from her father.
    Owing to the poor attendance, the Committee
decided to close the schools this afternoon until
January 2nd.

1896

January 2nd: Opened school on Thursday after the Christmas
Holidays. Clara Ironmonger commenced duties
as monitress.

January 24th: C. Ironmonger performs badly as an infant teacher. She has no energy and is altogether too slow.

January 31st: C. Ironmonger's month of probation having expired, had a talk to her about what I considered her incapability as an infant teacher. She was absent in the afternoon.

March 6th: Miss Holgate commenced duties as Assistant Mistress on March 2nd. Had to speak very strongly to Clara Ironmonger about smacking the children.

March 20th: Have taken Miss Holgate's class most of the week as she keeps very bad order. She works and talks away but never troubles whether the children are attending or not.

Clara Ironmonger makes little if any improvement in the art of teaching.

March 27th: Clara Ironmonger transferred to the girls' department.

April 8th: Report received (boys' department): 'The Boys are in very good order and their attainments are improving. Reading, Handwriting on paper and spelling still fall below a thoroughly good standard. The asphalt in the playground needs repairing.'

April 24th: Sent Tom W. home twice this week to have his clothes washed, as they were filthy dirty and the smell most offensive.

Received the following notice: 'My Lords have sanctioned on the special recommendation of Her Majesty's Inspector the omission of the annual inspection of the Infants Department of your school due in February 1897.'

May 8th: Mrs M. came to school very noisy and indignant on Wednesday afternoon in answer to a note I sent her asking her to wash Sydney's clothes as he smelt very disagreeable. She listened to reason and went away quiet, promising to attend to him.

June 6th: Wrote to the School Board with respect to Katy Holt, Probationer. Found her useful in school work, but her own studies are very weak indeed. Doubtful whether she could pass Standard Four; seeing she was sixteen in April, can see no prospect of her making a successful student.

June 26th: Schools closed on Thursday to enable teachers to visit the Royal Agricultural Show at Leicester.

July 10th: Sent S. Moore home on Monday. His sister having been away from school last week ill, the symptoms of which were certainly very much like scarlatina. The attendance visitor saw Dr Griffiths who said he certainly ought not to be at school.

W. Burton at school on Thursday afternoon and Friday all day. Before the Magistrates yesterday, parent fined 2*s* 6*d*. Had been at school twice since Whit week. The progress of such scholars is necessarily very slow, besides retarding that of the other scholars.

July 17th: Miss Orton away on Wednesday afternoon waiting on the Birmingham Board under which she has gained an appointment.

July 24th: On Wednesday morning at playtime, Tom King, three years old, put the hook used in fastening the door back in the playground into his mouth and cut his cheek badly. Had him at once taken to a doctor who attended to it. Is going on well. The hook has been removed and replaced and a lock put in its place.

July 31st: Have sent home eleven children suffering with mumps, telling the parents they must not return until quite well.

August 7th: May Reynolds granted a week's holiday to go to the seaside. This has caused a great deal of dissatisfaction amongst the other teachers.

August 14th: I took a holiday on Wednesday afternoon to go to Bosworth Flower Show.

Misses Orton and Toft resigned their positions as assistants in these schools.

October 2nd: A man called Taylor came to school on Tuesday afternoon very noisy and abusive saying that on Monday I had struck his boy across the face with a cane and left a weal, and they had only just seen it. This was totally untrue but he wouldn't listen and, as his language was very bad, I sent for a policeman when he became quieter and in a manner apologised. The boy certainly had a mark, but it was fresh done, and not at school. Had the appearance of a slash from a whip.

October 23rd: Miss Holmes absent all the week ill. I have taken her class.

October 30th: Miss Holmes returned to school on Monday apparently all right, but before school on Tuesday she was hysterical, saying she had sent in her resignation and could she go home at once. She gave as her reason that she was not strong enough for the work and couldn't do anything if she stayed. I advised her to see the Chairman as I had no power to grant her request, but this she refused to do, so I went and on returning found her gone.

December 3rd: Dale left the school at playtime, attendance cancelled. Not present in the afternoon. Since November 2nd this boy has made seven attendances out of a possible forty-nine. No wonder he is so behind with his work.

December 18th: Violet Hugill absent all the week. Attending the Scholarship Examination.

Aa Bb Cc Dd Ee Ff Gg

Hh Ii Jj Kk Ll Mm Nn

Oo Pp Qq Rr Ss Tt Uu

Vv Ww Xx Yy Zz

Children who blot their copy book will be severely punished!

Children were taught to write in a cursive style known as Copperplate. Victorians placed great importance on presentation and good handwriting skills, so children had to copy words over and over again to improve. This practise was done in a book called a copy book. Left-handed children were forced to use their right hand to avoid smudging the ink.

Six

End of an Era, 1897–1904

The Victorian age came to an end on January 22nd 1901, when Queen Victoria died at Osborne House on the Isle of Wight. Aged eighty-one, she had been Queen of England and Empress of India for over sixty-three years. She was succeeded by Edward VII.

1897

January 8th: School opened on January 4th with a very fair attendance. William Wood died of typhoid fever during the holidays.

January 21st: Schools closed for tomorrow in order that the rooms can be fumigated throughout.

February 5th: Miss Starbuck, Inspectress under the Leicester School Board, visited on Monday morning and examined Standard One and children fit to be transferred to the upper departments. Report received on Tuesday: 'The work of this class was very good, the writing being worthy of special mention.'

March 12th: Messrs Bott, Ironmonger, Taylor and Kiddle visited on Wednesday morning. At their request have decided to alter the style of writing taught in this department the last two or three years for the round style again, to suit the wishes of the teachers in the upper departments.

April 2nd: Miss V. Hugill received notice on Thursday that she had passed the Scholarship Examination and was placed in the Class Three.

April 9th: Lewis Wood died from burns received by falling on the fire while playing 'tip-tap' in the house.

April 27th: Readmitted John Brown. This boy has been at a Deaf and Dumb Institution, but for some reason has been sent home again.

April 30th: Schools reopened on Monday morning with a very fair attendance: 412 present. Seventy-four children admitted. Several returned after scarlatina and one, May Bennett, died in hospital during the holidays.

May 6th: Cox locked in school all dinnertime by his father's request. Continual truant playing. Have been very much troubled with truant players last week and this.

May 21st: Attendance poor all week. A few cases of measles reported.

Mrs Worthington came to school after twelve o'clock on Wednesday and again in the afternoon using threats and abusive language, because she said her boy had been sent out to wash his hands, and she had told him not to. He was very dirty though. She was in a great rage and wouldn't listen to reason so sent Mr Burton with a note telling her she must not come inside the school again without permission as her language was not fit for children to hear. Every few weeks she quite upsets the school for a little time, bursting in and storming at one or other of the teachers.

June 25th: On Monday each child was presented with a
                    Diamond Jubilee Commemoration Card and
                    thirty-five of the best attenders were presented
                    with medals. Schools closed on Tuesday and
                    Wednesday in celebration of the Queen's
                    Diamond Jubilee.

July 9th: Received from Baxters, four dozen packets of
                    good attendance cards.

July 16th: Mrs Saunders brought Gertrude to school on
                    Monday afternoon to complain of Miss Watson
                    having caned her in the morning and to show me
                    two welts, one on each arm. Called Miss Watson
                    to speak for herself. She said the girl was naughty
                    and she thought as I was working in the junior
                    department that she would punish her.
                        This is the second time she has used the cane
                    during my absence to the junior department, but
                    has promised not to do it again.

October 4th: Papers of Class Five, Standard Two not so very
                    satisfactory. Letters badly formed. Too much
                    ink used.

October 5th: Punished a boy for having some bad language on
                    his slate.

October 22nd: Two cases of scarlatina reported. Sent notes
                    to parents of irregular attenders asking for
                    improvement. The attendance of Friday morning
                    is always affected by boys staying away to sell
                    newspapers.

October 29th: Three fresh cases of scarlatina reported and one of
                    measles. Harry Townsend died of typhoid fever.
                        All absentees enquired after by the teachers.
                    Coughs, colds and bad throats seem to be the
                    principal causes of absence.

November 12th: Ethel Orton's mother came to ask me to put her in a lower class as she was a year younger than I thought. She gave the wrong age when she first brought her to school in June 1893, so that she might be admitted.

December 10th: Nellie Grove came to school on Tuesday morning after three weeks absence. On examination found that she was in the peeling stage after scarlatina. Sent her home at once with a note warning her mother of the danger.

1898

January 7th: Schools reopened with an improved attendance. Most of the children returned that had been away with scarlatina. Sent Nellie Grove and Lily Worthington home for doctor's certificates, as they had not been in hospital.

Readmitted Douglas Spencer. Has been away for several months with 'Saint Vitus Dance'.

William Fish was away on Tuesday and Wednesday and on examining him on Thursday found that he was in the peeling stage after scarlatina. Sent him home at once with a note and Mr Burton also informed Dr Griffiths of the case.

January 14th: Mabel Abbott has conducted her class in a very slipshod and slovenly manner since the holidays, and on speaking to her about it on Thursday, she answered quite insolently, saying she 'shouldn't try with that lot again' and didn't seem at all to mind the consequences of her behaviour.

February 3rd: Certificate given for Shaw. Made 32 attendances out of 114 since November 1st: father to appear before the Magistrates.

March 25th: Gave an object lesson on 'a clock face' instead of Mabel Abbott who 'forgot' to prepare either notes or lesson as requested.

April 1st: Attendance very poor owing to an epidemic of measles. Sent home all children from infected houses.

April 6th: Mrs Bedford called on Monday with respect to her son John. The doctor at the infirmary has ordered complete rest for his eyes for a month at least.

April 22nd: Schools reopened on Monday morning with a very poor attendance: 253 present out of a possible 500. In the boys' department, I find on going through the registers that fifty are away with measles. Fresh cases occurring daily. All rooms thoroughly disinfected and scoured during the holiday.

April 29th: Attendance no better; consequently, school work rather slow.
        Mabel Whiting and Maud Grewcock died from complications after measles.

July 15th: Punished George Geary at the request of his mother for playing truant the whole of Thursday and Friday in last week, and Monday.

1899

January 6th: Attendance good in most cases. Still there are a few who might put in full time. As a matter of course they are generally the ones who are the most backward.

January 13th: All absentees visited by myself and teachers: whooping cough, blister pox and colds the cause of absence in most cases.

Certificates, cash prizes and medals were awarded to
encourage good attendance. This Queen Victoria Medal from
the School Board for London was awarded to H. Harris for
punctual attendance during the school year ended 1899.

February 10th: New stock delivered including memory maps,
poetry cards, pencils and new Map of England.

April 18th: George Green (Class Six) returned to school. Last
attendance made February 23rd. Truant playing.
Father was summoned March 16th.

April 21st: Mr Burton reported two cases of scarlatina.
As Annie Bott and May Reynolds persisted in
not bringing their object lesson note books for
me to see, though repeatedly told to do so, I asked
the reason why, when they said it seemed absurd
that they should do so as they were no longer
pupil teachers. After a good deal of discussion and
dictatorial remarks from them, they promised to

do as I requested. I told them that if such a thing occurred again I should report the whole case to the Board. Mabel Abbott not present but has acted in the same defiant manner.

April 27th: Father of George Green (Class Six) before Magistrates for his son's irregularity from March 13th to April 25th (incl.). Attended five out of forty-nine: fined 5*s*.

May 10th: The father of George Green once again before the Magistrates. Fined 5*s*. Attended six out of eighteen times.

June 8th: George Green again before the Magistrates. Since May 12th has attended twelve out of twenty-six times: fined 5*s*.

June 23rd: Mabel Abbott neglected the last two weeks to write out notes for her object lesson. Excuse: she 'forgot to do them.' Each time wrote them out after the lesson had been given.
　A holiday given on Thursday afternoon, on the reason of the laying of the Foundation Stone of new Jubilee Cottage Hospital.

July 21st: Attendance has been poor this week. The recent hot weather no doubt accounts for colds, headaches &c. which are put up as excuses. Several boys have gone out of town for their holidays.

August 3rd: The present weather is very trying in school. The thermometer has been over 80°F several times.

September 8th: Refused admittance to William Fletcher on Monday morning as on examining his hands we found that he was peeling after scarlatina. This denied by mother but confirmed by Medical Officer of Health who sent him at once to the Scarlatina Hospital.

September 15th: No notes prepared by Mabel Abbott the last two weeks for her object lessons, consequently lessons given in a slipshod haphazard manner. Says she has lost her book and is going to write them all out together.

October 20th: Mr Watson and Mrs Williams visited on Wednesday afternoon. Enquired of them about a teacher in Miss Robottom's place as she is going to be married.

October 28th: Miss V. Hugill received notice on 26th October that she had obtained a Second and Third in the recent Certificate Examination, First Year's Papers.

December 1st: Attendance very irregular. Have sent home several children with bad throats and headache.

December 22nd: Miss V. Hugill resigned her position as assistant in these schools.

1900

January 12th: Ethel Summers absent all the week; very ill with peritonitis.

February 9th: Attendance poor all the week owing to the severity of the weather.

February 23rd: Many of the children are suffering from chilblains and not able to wear their boots.

March 1st: News to hand, Relief of Ladysmith.

March 23rd: Annie Morris met with a slight accident – forehead cut a little – in the playground on Thursday afternoon by running up against Miss Wills as she was ringing the bell.

May 18th: Gave a specimen sand-tray writing lesson to the babies and a number lesson to a Class of five-year-olds.

May 25th: A whole holiday given on Thursday to commemorate the relief of Mafeking and the Queen's Birthday.

July 20th: Only 294 present on Friday afternoon, owing to a severe thunderstorm.

September 14th: Mrs Williams and Mr Taylor came in on Wednesday morning with Mr Kiddle with reference to my request for nine dual desks. The need of them being seen the Clerk was instructed to order at once.

September 21st: Truant playing – found out several cases this week. Selling papers is again the excuse of a few.

Hinckley Board School logbook in use until 1914.

October 5th: Nine new dual desks received from the Midland
                      Educational Company, Birmingham.

November 13th: James Knight (Class Four, Standard Two)
                      returned to school. Been travelling with his father
                      round about since April 27th. This boy's age is
                      given as twelve in June last. Doubtful whether he
                      could pass Standard One exam.

1901

January 19th   Hinckley Grammar School announced that it was
                      to become a mixed school, opening its doors for the
                      first time for girls to attend. Special arrangements
                      had been made to accommodate them. School fees:
                      Under-twelve years of age: £1 6s 8d per term.
                      Children over twelve years of age: £2 per term.

February 15th: Dr Jenkins, Medical Officer of Health, visited
                      on Monday morning to enquire as to number of
                      children absent and cause, as there is an outbreak
                      of measles in the Coventry Road and Trinity Lane
                      parts of the town.

February 22nd: Mrs Mills came to school at quarter past twelve
                      on Wednesday morning and was most abusive to
                      Miss Needham because she had kept Nellie in for
                      a little time for disobedience. Kept the girl away in
                      the afternoon so sent Mr Burton after her. Found
                      her nursing the baby and mother full of excuses.

March 15th: All absentees visited. Three cases of measles found but
                      principal cause of absence is still blister or chicken pox.

March 22nd: Sent home three children suffering with
                      ringworms. Notice received form the Clerk that
                      a doctor's certificate must be brought before any
                      child is readmitted after ringworm, sore head

or any infectious disease. If not from their own doctor they may be sent to Dr Jenkins and the Board will pay for it. Notice put up in school.

George Mills absent for over a week reason given toothache. Returned on Wednesday afternoon when it was found he had had measles and was still poorly. I sent him home and visited the mother warning her of the danger to other children as Alfred had been in school all the time. Excused herself by saying she had thought it couldn't be measles as the rash only came out on his legs and body and he had had a swollen face.

April 5th: A few more cases of measles reported. Total number of children away with or on account of having this disease in the house: sixteen.

April 26th: Twenty-one boys have been absent all week. The majority of these are excluded either for measles in the family or for ringworm.

May 3rd: Measles increasing every day consequently attendance poor.

May 10th: Dr Jenkins visited on Thursday morning to see how measles were affecting us: 125 cases at the present time and thirteen of ringworm.

May 17th: One case of diphtheria reported, Elsie Buswell, and one whooping cough, Ernest Crow. Measles increasing daily: 171 away owing to this disease only.

May 24th: A few children returned after measles and more fallen. Attendance poor on Thursday afternoon, owing to a procession of returned volunteers through the town.

June 21st: There are twenty-four children still absent through measles and fifteen through ringworm.

July 31st: Sent Morris (Class Two) home at playtime in
                    the morning. Climbing on the beams of the shed
                    and fell on his wrist. Heard after that his wrist
                    was broken. Spoke to the teachers as to keeping a
                    sharper lookout in the playground.

September 6th: Schools disinfected during the holidays. A holiday
                    given on Tuesday afternoon to allow the children to
                    visit Wombwell's Menagerie which was in town.

September 13th: Attendance not so good. A good many cases of
                    whooping cough reported amongst the young ones.
                    One case of scarlatina.

September 27th: Mrs Worthington came to school at three
                    thirty-five on Wednesday afternoon and used very
                    abusive and threatening language to Miss Cave
                    for thrashing her Albert. She said he went home
                    crying and was so sick that he was then lying
                    on the sofa and couldn't raise his head and that
                    she should have to sit up with him all night.
                    Miss Cave denied thrashing or even had occasion
                    to speak to him during the morning, but she
                    wouldn't listen to a word.

                    On going home at twenty past three, Miss Cave
                    met the boy coming back from blackberrying and
                    next morning on being questioned said he had not
                    told his mother he had been thrashed and that
                    he had not been sick or hit, that she kept him at
                    home to go errands. When he had done these he
                    went down Holly Croft.

October 4th: Reported Mrs Worthington's case to the Board who
                    instructed the Clerk to send her a letter of warning.

October 11th: William Robinson returned to school on Thursday;
                    he's been away since February 21st with ringworm.
                    Sent Maud Butterworth home as she seemed in pain
                    from a skin disease which affects her whole body.

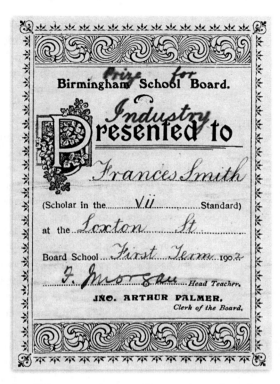

Birmingham *Prize* School *for* Board.

Industry

Presented to

Frances Smith

(Scholar in the ....*VII*........ Standard)

at the ....*Loxton*.... *St*

Board School ....*First Term*.... 190*2*

....*F. Morgan*.... Head Teacher.

JNO. ARTHUR PALMER.
Clerk of the Board.

In addition to attendance, certificates, prizes and awards encouraged children to try harder. Frances Smith was awarded this 'Prize for Industry' by the Birmingham School Board in 1902.

November 19th: Readmitted James and Will Knight. Parents have a caravan and wander from town to town in summer. Boys get a few months schooling in the winter.

1902

January 17th: On Tuesday afternoon Elsie Steel got locked in school. How? No one knows. She went out at five past four with her class and nothing more was seen of her until Mr Burton found her when he came to attend to the stoves at seven o'clock, sitting in a desk fast asleep. She told him she couldn't find her cap and when we were all gone she tried the door and then sat down and went to sleep.

Before leaving at twenty-five past four a tour of the rooms was made but no one was in. A teacher turned out the gas in the cloakroom and saw no one.

On hearing of it the next morning, I was on my road to see the mother when I met her coming to see me. She was naturally very angry but when I told her how sorry we were it had happened and that we were as innocent as she was, she came round and was quite reasonable and said she should send her to school in the afternoon as it hadn't hurt her.

As she didn't come then nor the next day and had been seen by children in the Walk, I went to enquire after her. She said she had altered her mind about sending her and then the language was so bad that I couldn't stop in the house.

January 24th: Mrs Steel came to school on Monday morning in a great fury falsely accusing Miss Needham of caning Elsie when she kept her at home. Her language was so filthy and threatening that I sent for a policeman but she left before one came vowing to waylay this teacher and 'kill her'.

February 7th: Miss Needham received an apology from Mrs Steel and also withdrawal of all accusations of caning and ill-treatment to her child Elsie.

April 18th: Sergeant Lockton and Mr John Harrold came to school on Friday afternoon and asked for Sam Hincks, Sam Armstrong (absent), Will Vallance, Kie Brown, Walter Farmer and Jos Norton for breaking windows and doing other damage to an empty factory. The policeman frightened them to such an extent with the handcuffs and his staff that I refused his request

to take them and lock them up. They were in
such a fearful state that I was afraid something
serious might happen.

May 2nd: Attendance poor all week. A good many children
away with swollen faces caused through colds,
and a few with chicken pox.

May 9th: Taught the children the National Anthem and
began to teach a Coronation Hymn.

May 30th: A few more absent this week on account of blister
pox in the home.

June 6th: A holiday given on Monday to celebrate the Peace
Proclamation.

June 20th: Admitted two children: six and seven years old. Have
not been to school before and do not know a letter.

June 25th: Teachers of various classes explained the meaning
and construction of the Union Jack. Schools
to be closed tomorrow (Thursday) and Friday.
The arrangements with regard to the Coronation
are to be carried out as regards the children:
procession in afternoon, tea after, and each child is
to receive a Coronation Mug.

July 18th: Walter Farmer met with an accident on Monday
afternoon when marching into the classroom.
Fell and caught his cheek on the edge of a form,
causing a black eye.

August 1st: Mrs Williams and Mr Cox visited on Tuesday
morning and I again pointed out the need of a
piano for the junior department and also wrote
to the Board on the same subject. Brought the
case of William Grantham, a deaf and dumb boy,
to their notice.

September 26th: William Grantham, the deaf and dumb boy, left to attend the Roman Catholic School with a view to getting into one of their institutions. Bert Hewins returned to school; been absent since April 1901 with ringworm.

October 3rd: Nellie Saunders returned after ringworm; been away since April.

1903

January 30th: Mrs Williams and Messrs Bott, Freeman, Kiddle (Clerk) and Lee (Gas-Manager) visited on Tuesday morning and arranged to put incandescent lights in all the rooms.

February 6th: Gave a pencil to all junior boys who have attended all week.

February 27th: Joseph Bailey died from inflammation of the kidneys.

March 6th: Have been unable to use classrooms in the junior department this week. Builders taking windows out to build staircase in new school.

March 20th: Mr Freeman and Mr Bott visited on Tuesday afternoon to see what can be done to the classroom in the junior department to make it lighter. Now that the windows have been bricked up the room is very unpleasant to work in.

May 15th: Sent home two children with ringworm. George B. gone into the workhouse for a fortnight while his mother is in prison.

June 12th: I asked Mr Kiddle to write to Mrs C., warning her against using bad language to and about the teachers. She is in the habit of coming to school,

threatening and using filthy language and making
all sorts of false accusations against any teacher
she may happen to see.

June 19th: Worthington was before the Magistrates
yesterday for his boy Alfred (Class Six). Since
May 26th has been sixty-four out of a possible
ninety-four: fined 2s 6d.

June 26th: A new piano received on Thursday afternoon.

June 29th: School Board as such ceases to exist today.

July 1st: Schools now carried on under the auspices of the
Leicestershire County Council in accordance with
the Education Act 1902.

July 31st: Took the opportunity to speak of the growing
practice of some junior boys staying away two or
more times each week. Told them that the new
authority would certainly prosecute in cases of
inadequate attendance.

September 11th: Schools reopened on Monday morning after
five weeks holiday. An extension of one week
given, due to schools not being ready owing
to alterations.
        Mr Kiddle visited on Thursday morning.
Asked him to write to Educational Secretary
about foolscap for use of children applied for
early in July.

September 18th: Have had to use slates for writing lessons most of
the week. No foolscap sent, nor news of any.

September 25th: Sent Walter Adcock home on Tuesday afternoon
as found his hands peeling, evidently after a
fever. He was away the week after holidays with a
feverish cold as certified by the doctor, and returned

on 14th September apparently alright. Reported the case to the Medical Officer of Health, and also disinfected slates that had been used in the class.

No news of foolscap. Still using slates.

Attendance rather irregular owing to the Wild West Show in Leicester and a local 'Wake'.

October 2nd: Attendance very poor owing to an epidemic of measles: 106 children up to Friday away with or through this disease. Dr Jenkins Medical Officer of Health visited on Wednesday afternoon to see how we were affected.

October 9th: Received twelve reams foolscap from the Midland Educational Depot. The handwriting has suffered owing to using slates the last few weeks.

Measles on the increase and two more cases of scarlatina sent to the hospital.

October 30th: Henry Allsop died on Wednesday, was recovering from measles when he was seized with vomiting and collapsed.

November 6th: Eileen Granger died on November 1st from bronchial pneumonia followed by measles.

November 20th: Playground freshly asphalted.

November 27th: Have had to punish Florence F. several times this week for thieving and lying. I have written to the mother telling her of the habit and consequences that must follow, but she makes light of it. Nothing is safe from this child.

December 11th: Mr Aucott and Mr Kinton visited on Monday morning to look through the schools and to get the average attendance for November. Spoke to them about the difficulties of the out offices being so far from the school.

1904

January 29th: Miss Payne absent all the week. Telegraphed for on Monday morning, to go to sister who had been badly burnt and from which she died on Wednesday night.

Mr Biggs and Mr Ironmonger visited on Tuesday morning. Asked them for a new stove for the large room in the junior department; the old one is worn out and cannot be used.

Average attendance for year: 501.6.

February 12th: The Director of Education, along with members of the School Management Committee, visited on Tuesday morning. I asked for pictures in Drill Hall and furniture for Teachers' Room.

February 19th: Messrs Langham, Taylor and Kiddle visited the junior department on Tuesday morning to inspect the old stove prior to ordering a new one.

March 1st: The severe and changeable weather has materially affected the average this week. Many junior boys have been absent all week; colds or bad feet with chilblains has been a frequent excuse.

March 11th: The new thermometer placed in the Drill Hall found broken.

April 26th: Report received (boys' department):

The classes are of convenient sizes, but have worked at considerable disadvantage owing to the overcrowded state of the school. Their condition, generally speaking, reflects credit on the members of the staff.

April 29th: Miss Bott absent on Friday. Brought a doctor's certificate during the week to say a change of air would be beneficial; has gone to the seaside for a week or two.

May 6th: On Wednesday William Sparrow was found in the playground by the teachers at quarter to nine in the morning, crying. Said he had pinched his finger in the school door. As it was badly cut I took him to the doctor who dressed it. His teacher took him home and explained it to his mother.

May 20th: Miss Needham sent in her resignation, owing to her approaching marriage.

June 3rd: Miss Horspool absent all week. Doctor's certificate to say 'she is suffering from a poisoned finger'.

July 22nd: Admitted four children, three between the ages of six and seven, and one between seven and eight. Two had never been inside a school before and the other two only a few times. No idea of letters. Their excuse was that they were refused admittance at Nuneaton, all schools full.

July 29th: Parents of Horace Orton (Class Six) were summoned yesterday and fined 5*s* for irregular attendance.

September 12th: Admitted Jos Brown, date of birth March 27th 1895. Been living in Nuneaton but has not been at school; does not know his letters.

November 4th: Dr Robinson, Medical Officer of Health to the County Council, visited on Wednesday afternoon to enquire into cases of mentally deficient children.
 Fetched a policeman on Friday afternoon, as Florence Hill's purse was taken off the stove in the morning while she was putting on a child's jacket: Sam Daniels, Uriah Crofts and Ernest Baker implicated. Found out that S. Daniels took it and went to different shops spending 4*d* in all,

This certificate was awarded to Robert Blease, a pupil in the
Steers Street School, Liverpool, for 'Regularity and Punctuality
of Attendance and for General Good Conduct' January 1905.

the other boys accompanying him as they saw
him take it. 1*d* found in his pocket. The purse and
remainder 1*d* traced to Daniels' father, to whom
the boy passed it. Policeman found the man who
gave it up. I punished the other two boys for not
informing teachers and Daniels for stealing it.

November 11th: Mrs Daniels brought 4*d* and returned it to
Florence Hill and asked her to forgive her boy and
husband. No further proceedings to be taken.
    Filled up and returned forms to Education
Office of names of mentally deficient and
dull children.

November 18th: Several boys away because of measles, whooping
cough or chicken pox being in the family or
suffering themselves from colds. The recent very
severe weather is very trying to those who are clad
well and must be intensely so to some of the others.

November 25th: Whooping cough increasing. Scarcely a day passes
but what I have to send children home suffering
from it. Am excluding all when they have it in
their house.

Seven

Want of Boots, 1905–1913

Overcrowding, disease and poverty continue to have a marked effect on the school. Winter conditions were particularly difficult for children who were inadequately dressed. Some were unable to attend during periods of bad weather having no suitable footwear. These children are marked as absent through 'want of boots'.

1905

February 4th: Report: 'The children are taught kindly and with creditable success. The teachers have some special difficulties to contend with in the matter of accommodation for the many large classes and because of the home circumstances of many of the children. These difficulties are met with a good spirit.'

February 10th: Mr Freeman at the school on Monday morning last, to give prizes for attendance. Showed him list I had prepared and made suggestions.

March 31st: Filled up and returned the Quarterly Returns of Attendances to the office, also a new weekly return of children away with or through any infectious disease or bad heads.

April 20th: Prizes for attendance given out:

First prize: full attendance (434) and not late	3s 6d	8 children
Second prize: 420 to 433 and not late	2s 6d	27 children
Third prize: full attendance but late	2s	9 children
Fourth prize: under 433 but late	1s	51 children

April 21st: On Monday morning I found Esther Dixon's hands peeling and took her to the Medical Officer who said she had evidently had scarlatina. Three weeks ago she was away for a week with a cold but had been in school since: was sent to the Isolation Hospital in the afternoon.

May 18th: The parents of Orton (Class Three) summoned for irregular attendance, 83 out of 112: fined *7s 6d*.

June 9th: Measles on the increase. Fresh cases reported every day.

June 23rd: Measles increasing rapidly: thirty cases on Wednesday; sixty-eight reported by Friday. Admitted Jesse Ford from Nuneaton, nearly thirteen years old. Has not been in any school for about two years.

July 7th: Twenty children returned after measles but forty fresh cases during the week.

July 14th: Twenty-four children returned after measles. Eighty-one cases at the present time away.

July 21st: The results of the recent exam have been very much affected by the irregular attendance during some weeks for measles &c. One lot gets back and others have to be excluded so that one is not always safe teaching fresh rules, especially in arithmetic.

WARWICKSHIRE COUNTY COUNCIL
EDUCATION COMMITTEE.

School.....*Fentham Road*..............

Name.....*Arthur Chandler*..............

Period.....*January* .... *190 6*.

Never Absent, Never Late.

Reward-of-Merit tickets were given out as early as the
middle of the nineteenth century. On one side there was a
printed picture and on the other side details of the nature
of the award. These tickets are thought to be the very first
collectable card, it being possible to collect a complete 'set'.

November 3rd: On Tuesday morning transferred twenty boys to
the boys' department and twelve girls to the girls';
Mr and Mrs Heaton not being able to take any
more through lack of room.

December 22nd: Three fresh cases of scarlatina. One John Wilby
died the day after being sent to the hospital.

1906

January 19th: Fire out in Classroom Two on Monday morning
when class sent in at half past nine. I sent for Iliffe
(caretaker) to ask him to come and light it at once
and went to him myself at eleven o'clock, but he
didn't come near till after twelve.

February 9th: Forms of one sort or another keep coming in: these take up a great deal of time.

February 16th: Sent two boys home this afternoon on account of the condition of their clothes. Had previously asked attendance visitor to call. The attention of the Committee on Tuesday was called to these boys. Names entered on doctor's form.

April 27th: Mr Ironmonger and Mr H. Kiddle visited on Tuesday. HM Inspector, who was paying a Visit of Inspection at the time, called their attention to the dirty state of the walls, windows, stoves &c. in the junior department and asked that the caretaker be informed of the same.

Admitted two boys today, one nearly eleven and the other nine. Neither of them could do Standard One work. Live in a caravan; here for a week or two.

May 3rd: Boothe (Class One) playing in yard before nine o'clock, was knocked down and his leg broken. Sent up to Dr Stanley. Afterwards, Simpkins and Iliffe (caretaker) took him to Cottage Hospital.

May 18th: Mr Freeman and Mr Kinton visited on Tuesday morning. Decided that no child under four to be admitted until after July, as the babies' room is so full.

June 15th: Still a difficulty to get all the little ones in time for register (quarter past nine in the morning): nine or ten marked absent each morning. A good many of the mothers work at the factories and find it impossible in the half hour allowed for breakfast to get all ready in time.

August 3rd: Florence Hill completed her apprenticeship as a pupil teacher on July 31st and taken on as Assistant Art. Fifty on August 1st.

September 14th: Another fresh case of scarlatina. At the present time there are five away with this disease; five with ringworm; four with sores in the head and one with measles.

September 21st: Attendance not so good. All absentees visited by teachers: colds and toothache the reason given in most cases. One fresh case of scarlatina and one boy kept away owing to mother having it.

On Tuesday sent out a note to Mrs M. asking her to wash John's clothes as they were very dirty. This she did but he was just as bad on Friday.

September 28th: Dr Robinson visited on Thursday morning. I pointed out to him two children of weak intellect but he said nothing had been settled yet about such cases.

October 19th: Miss W. Jackson received notice, together with a list of vacancies, to find a post in another school as this is over-staffed. Gave her a testimonial.

November 6th: HM Inspector's Report (Boys' Department):

This Department has not yet freed itself from the methods of work which prevailed in it when work was carried on under the difficulties of crowded rooms, with children from poor homes, and with an eye to an annual examination. Some of these difficulties (the adverse home circumstances of many of the children and the fact that three classes are taught in the main room which is a passage room to the classrooms) still persist, but the conditions have so far improved that progress in the character and efficiency of the work should be more distinctly evident. For thoroughly good teaching, it is necessary that the children should be spoken to clearly, fairly and, as a rule, gently; and that they should be trained in the habit of speaking out clearly and intelligently. The weak point, amid a good deal of conscientious work, is that the attention of the boys is not attracted and retained with full success, hence a certain restlessness and half attention which hinders progress.

The Infants' School, which has more than 500 children towards the end of the school year, consists of two sections in different buildings. It is divided into nine or ten classes. The first five classes are taught in one building the lower classes in the other. A room known as the 'Drill Hall' is also used.

The building in which the younger children are taught consists of a large room in which are three classes separated by curtains, a classroom and a baby room. The teaching of three large classes in an undivided room is always a difficult matter and the difficulty is increased when the number of children is so large that three sit in a dual desk.

The children in this section of the school are so young that their instruction in reading, writing and arithmetic is less important than training in intelligent listening and speaking and suitable occupations and games. The want of space and the crowding of the desks make conversational lessons and occupations very difficult, and prevent the teachers attaining to and, if they have had no experience in more fortunate schools, from understanding what may be done to help the development of the children's faculties under more favourable conditions.

The children, however, are kindly managed and so far as the circumstances and the opportunities of the teachers allow they are efficiently taught.

The upper section of the Infants' School has a large room in which two of the three classes are taught and two classrooms. The large room is a passage room to one of the classrooms. The larger classroom is not furnished with desks. It is desirable that desks should be provided. In this section also the teachers work under difficulties. By much diligence they maintain the efficiency of the school, but the amenity of the school both for teachers and children is diminished by the cramping nature of the accommodation and the progress of the children is slower than it would be under more favourable conditions.

The headmistress, who takes her full share of hard work, has practically the supervision of two departments. She meets her difficulties cheerfully and is well seconded by the diligence and loyalty of the staff. Great care is given to the training of pupil teachers.

Openings in the lower parts of the windows are desirable.

November 16th: Messrs Freeman, Ironmonger and Kiddle visited on Tuesday morning and made enquiries as to the number of desks required for Classroom One.

Awarded to Robert Linscott by the Plymouth Education Authority, for 'Good Attendance' during the year ended May 31st 1906. The certificate records that he attended 385 times out of a possible 425.

1907

February 14th: Conference after morning school with the staff. Head spoke strongly, and let us hope efficiently, as to cultivating the 'Teacher's Eye' &c.

March 1st: Have taken off the register the names of nine children under five, owing to irregularity.

March 15th: The girls in the mixed school have been very annoying as usual during playtime, running up and down the passages, cloakrooms and Drill Hall steps. On Friday, seven or eight shut themselves in the babies' cloakroom and made a great noise. I sent for their teacher who promised to punish them. Have complained many times without satisfaction and the only way of keeping them outside is to lock the doors and this is most inconvenient.

March 29th: Attendance is falling off: fresh cases of mumps each day. Have sent four children home with the complaint.

April 12th: Examined each child each day as to fitness for school and found twenty on Tuesday morning, eight in the afternoon and one on Wednesday morning, with mumps. Sent them home. Forty-seven at the present with this disease and several others with colds.

May 3rd: Called the caretakers attention to boys' closets.

May 17th: Bertie Goodman's overcoat was taken from school and after making searching enquiries found out from the children that Charles Ford had taken one home. I sent for it and though it was fetched from upstairs was told, 'I thought he had brought it back.'

John M. so filthy and smelt so disgusting on Friday morning that I was obliged to send him home; I gave him a note for his mother telling her why – the second I have sent this week. As a rule he is quite unfit to be in school.

June 21st: On Friday morning, called Mr Burton's attention to the miserable condition owing to neglect of Florence and Sydney S. to see if he could do anything in the matter.

July 5th: While playing games in the Drill Hall on Monday morning, Bertie Smith fell and bruised his forehead. Had on new boots.

Messrs Freeman, Green and Kiddle visited on Tuesday morning and discussed the advisability of requiring Birth Certificates for fresh admissions to prevent children under four being admitted.

September 6th: Boy (Brown) brought his attendance paper. Birth Certificate shows his birthday to be October 31st. The boy said, 'It was wrong.' Told him to come again when he is thirteen.

September 20th: A case of typhoid fever, child not been to school since the holidays.

October 11th: The Inspector of Prevention of Cruelty to Children visited on Wednesday afternoon and had a talk with Minnie and Annie W., May B. and Mabel B.

October 18th: Sent Ford (Class Five) home on Wednesday. His mother called on Thursday morning to say 'there was nothing the matter with the boy' and she was taking him to Dr Jenkins. Have heard no more of it. The boy certainly had a louse on his jacket when sent away.

November 1st: The Inspector of Prevention of Cruelty to Children visited on Wednesday morning. He had boots for the B. children.

November 15th: On Friday morning I sent home a girl full of measles and also took Winifred B. to the Medical Officer of Health as she had a suspicious looking disease on her hands and arms. Certified suffering from itch. I burnt all the pencils in use in the class.

December 6th: Mrs Reed, and later in the week Mrs Pratt, came to school and complained of finding vermin on their boys Alexander and Herbert, and asking who they had been sitting against. Showed each one

the class children were in and they were satisfied
that all looked clean. Had a talk to the whole
school afterwards on cleanliness.

1908

January 7th: In the absence of Miss Heaton, her class has been
taken during the week by her brother, who is here
on his holidays.

The 1906 Education Act empowered Local Education
Authorities to provide free school meals. In 1946, Parliament
passed the 'School Milk Act'. This Act ordered the issue of
one-third of a pint of milk free to all pupils under eighteen.

February 28th: Sent Edward and Ben B. home on Thursday morning as I found they were suffering from an infectious skin disease. The Medical Officer of Health visited on Friday afternoon and sent home Florence H. for the same thing.

May 1st: Walter Foster returned to school on Thursday morning after truanting wholly since April 10th, and on and off since March 20th.

May 15th: Punished Walter Foster on Tuesday and Wednesday mornings for truanting.

May 22nd: Walter Foster played truant on Monday and Wednesday afternoons. I punished him on Thursday morning at the request of his mother.

May 29th: Walter Foster truanting on Monday and Wednesday afternoons and the whole of Thursday.

June 5th: Walter Foster brought to school at twenty past two on Friday afternoon without coat or cap and very dirty. Had not been in school since Wednesday morning, when the managers talked to him about what would happen unless he came regularly to school.

June 19th: Miss Mills, owing to her approaching marriage, resigned her position as assistant.

June 26th: Walter Foster truanting on Monday afternoon and on Wednesday afternoon. The attendance officer found him in the street and brought him to school.

September 25th: Had several truants break out this week. Locked Morris in school all dinnertime on Thursday by request of his mother.

November 6th: At the present time, thiry-one are away with whooping cough, nine with chicken pox, two mumps, one scarlatina, five ringworm and others with colds and coughs.

Revd J. Woolerton, Mr Kinton and Mr H. Kiddle visited on Tuesday morning. I called their attention to Charles G. (a mentally deficient) and asked if anything could be done for him, as he has such dirty habits. Left till Dr Robinson can pay a visit.

Sent John M. home on Thursday morning to have his clothes washed. Was filthy.

November 13th: Sent Charles G. home on Friday morning as he was too filthy to be in school.

December 11th: The inclement weather has affected the average. Had two cases of boys not attending through want of boots.

December 18th: Have had to send Charles G. home four times this week for filthiness, he is quite unfit to be with other children.

Several children away on wet days owing to bad boots.

1909

February 5th: Medical Inspector visited on Wednesday and Friday and examined all children admitted since August 1st 1908. Advised that three children suffering from phthisis (tuberculosis) be excluded.

Hilda Mason died on Friday from heart disease and pneumonia. Had been away from school for some time.

February 19th: Colds still very prevalent. Had a few cases of boys having to stay away on account of measles in the house.

March 5th: Schools closed on Thursday morning,
twelve o'clock, by Medical Authority until 20th
inst. on account of epidemic of measles.

April 23rd: School reopened on Tuesday morning having
been closed since March 4th owing to continued
epidemic of measles.

May 14th: A good many children away half or whole days
with toothache or other minor ailments.
    Alfred Sanders, when going home out of school
on Wednesday afternoon, fell on one of the iron
mats and cut his face badly. Have had it removed.

June 21st: Began this week the new Scheme of Religious
Instruction as supplied by the LCC.

July 2nd: Susan Bailey, nearly five years old, accidentally
killed on Wednesday afternoon soon after
leaving school.

July 9th: Punished Alfred and Joseph Towers for taking
sweets out of a little boy's pocket.

July 16th: Inspector for Prevention of Cruelty to Children
visited on Tuesday morning and after seeing May
and Ada E. advised that they be excluded from
school until cleaner. Said they were in a verminous
condition and he would inform the mother.

September 3rd: Inspector for Prevention of Cruelty to Children
visited and looked at Tom B. who was in a dirty
and uncared for condition. Said he would see the
parents. Boy been cleaner since.

October 1st: Admitted a very delicate girl nearly ten years old.
Only been in a school six weeks owing to having
had spinal complaint meningitis &c. School
Medical Officer, Leicester, advised mother only to

let her attend an Infant's School for a time, as he feared if she were pushed at all it would affect her brain. Her sister, seven, delicate too, began school the same time; is only fit for this department.

Four children away all week because they have no boots.

October 8th: Two boys were run over: James Pope by motor cycle, hurt badly, and Fred Farmer by dray.

November 26th: Medical Inspector, Dr Blundell, visited on Friday morning and went amongst children in the Class Three noting dirty heads &c.

December 3rd: Messrs Freeman, Kinton and H. Kiddle visited on Tuesday morning and decided to have two inverted incandescent light put in the teacher's room for convenience of Medical Inspector.

1910

January 14th: Sent three children home with mumps and four with sores on face.

Discovered on Friday afternoon that Doris Bassford's hands were peeling. Sent her at once with teacher to Dr Jenkins, who said it was scarlatina. I took the child to mother and sent her to doctor for instructions as he advised. Child sent to Isolation Hospital during the afternoon. Disinfected pencils &c. in use in the class, and burnt papers and crayons.

February 4th: Sydney Herbert died in the Cottage Hospital on January 31st.

February 11th: Granted Miss Summers a part of Thursday afternoon to attend the opening of the new Trinity Church.

March 11th: Sent notes to parents of Walter M., Leslie S. and Percy G. asking them to wash their clothes and send them cleaner to school. They are all so filthy at times as to be quite unfit to be in school: a little improvement since.

March 18th: Punished Wilfred Taylor and Leslie Payne for truanting on Wednesday afternoon.

March 25th: Had to send Percy G. back again on Monday morning to wash himself.

April 8th: Attendance suffered on Wednesday afternoon owing to Sanger's Circus being in the town.
Had to send – again – to parents of Leslie S. and Alfred T. as they smelt very badly: cleaner since.

April 29th: Readmitted George Blower, though over eight years old. Mr Heaton declined to take him as all classes full he said. Played truant all day on Wednesday.
Transferred Beryl Granger to Girls' School: got too big for infants' desks.

May 6th: Transferred children from each class upwards: making a special class of backward ones, which I have taken all the week.

May 13th: Dr Jenkins visited on Wednesday morning and excluded George H. from school until free from infectious skin disease from which he is suffering. Pencils &c. used in his class thoroughly disinfected.

June 3rd: Sent a note to Mrs M. on Thursday morning asking her to wash Walter's clothes as he was quite unfit to sit against any child: has been absent since.

June 10th: Punished Leslie Mandley on Thursday afternoon for taking two cards of wool out of the school window and for truanting.

June 24th: Francis Gill's overcoat taken out of cap room on Wednesday afternoon. The next morning I traced it to John Palmer and fetched it back. Called at police station to see superintendent, who thought the best plan would be to send a policeman to fetch the boy and see what he could do with him. This was done. When boy returned to school seemed to treat it as a joke. So many different things have disappeared lately that I thought this would be a warning.

July 1st: Messrs Bennett, Cholerton, Kinton and Kiddle visited on Tuesday morning. I asked for new blinds for windows in junior department and also that a ventilator or opening of some kind be made, opposite to windows, in Classroom Two.

July 15th: Dr Jenkins, Medical Officer of Health and Mr Crump, Surveyor, visited on Monday afternoon and went into each room noting open windows, lavatory accommodation &c.

September 2nd: School reopened on Tuesday morning. Admitted nineteen children, ten left during the holidays and one, Marjorie Robinson, died.

September 16th: Punished Jesse Everitt on Thursday for truanting three times. Went off with Wilfred Taylor.

September 30th: On Friday afternoon, Miss Iliffe, owing to her approaching marriage, resigned her position as Assistant Mistress.

November 11th: Inspector for Prevention of Cruelty to Children visited on Tuesday morning to enquire if any cases required attention. Reported none.

> Hilda Nicholls taken to Isolation Hospital with diphtheria.

November 25th: On Friday morning Mrs T. came to school and was very abusive to Miss Summers over her treatment to her boy. She had taken him home again so I visited the house after school and left a message to ask the mother to bring him in the afternoon and see me about it. Neither she nor the boy came.

December 2nd: Mrs T. brought Eric back on Monday morning and we thrashed the question out.

The King's Medal was awarded by the London County Council to E. Katz for 'Punctual Attendance during the year 1910–1911 and three previous years'.

1911

January 13th: Punished James Neal at the request of his mother for lying and truanting.

January 20th: Wilfred Huckles, after playing truant since the holidays, was in school on Tuesday and Wednesday mornings but slipped away from his teacher at playtime both days and been absent since: is wandering about eluding both parents and policeman until ten or eleven o'clock at night.

January 27th: A man brought Wilfred Huckles to school on Thursday afternoon at quarter past three. Talked to him and he promised to come regularly in the future. In school both times on Friday.

March 3rd: Miss J. Clarke was so unfit for work on Tuesday morning owing to a gathering in her head that I sent her home again. Has been away since.

April 7th: All absentees visited by myself or teachers. Five fresh cases of mumps, two chicken pox, one diphtheria and two children excluded on account of measles in the house.

April 14th: Complained to Mr Whatmore again about the boys in mixed school spitting on the Drill Hall steps from over the railings in the corridor. Promised to see into it. It has become quite a nuisance the last few weeks.

Only 300 children present on account of a tea being given at three o'clock for poor children (Buffaloes).

April 28th: Took Fred F. to Medical Officer of Health, who certified him suffering from scabies and excluded him from school.

May 5th: Attendance decreased as week advanced. Mumps
increased daily: ninety-eight children away with
or on account of infectious diseases.

May 12th: Notice received from the Sanitary Authority
(CC) on May 13th that these schools be closed on
account of epidemic of chicken pox, measles and
mumps until May 27th.

    A further notice received on May 25th not to
reopen until after the Whitsuntide Holidays.

June 16th: Sixty-eight children away with infectious
diseases: forty-nine measles, seven mumps, four
chicken pox, three blister pox, four ringworm and
one scabies.

    Tom B. sent home in the morning suffering
from mumps. The boy is not in a fit state to be in
contact with other children. The nurse called in
school a short time afterwards so asked her to call
and see parents.

    School closed for one week's holiday to
celebrate Coronation of George V.

July 11th: Got the Medical Officer to examine Leslie French
and Percy G.'s eyes.

July 21st: Two fresh cases of measles reported, one of
scarlatina and two children excluded owing to a
case of typhoid in the house.

    Four children, on advice of Medical
Inspector, undergone operation for adenoids
and tonsils.

September 15th: Dr Wood, School Medical Officer, visited on
Tuesday morning and looked at several children
whose parents had not carried out instructions
given over a year ago.

    One death, Gladys Pratt, from scarlatina
and three fresh cases reported and two of

chicken pox. Sent May Wykes home with sores in the head. Dr Jenkins excluded Sarah and Florence Brookes and Hilda Woodward suffering from ringworm.

September 22nd: Mrs Foster came to school on Tuesday afternoon and was most abusive both to me and Miss Hill and threatening all sorts of things. Said the latter hit Harriet with a reading book on Friday afternoon and her head was full of sores in consequence. No books used in the class that afternoon and teacher is quite sure she never hit the child at all.

October 6th: Received notice that when a child returns from Isolation Hospital, all children from that house shall be excluded from school for a fortnight.

October 13th: So many children complained of bad throats on Monday afternoon that I sent to the doctor and asked if he would come and see what was wrong. Dr Jenkins out but Dr Donnell came. Out of forty examined, excluded twelve for the next week.

October 20th: Dr Jenkins M.O.H. visited on Tuesday morning and ordered the schools to be closed at twelve o'clock for three weeks on account of the prevalence of scarlet fever.

Ivy Adcock died in Isolation Hospital of scarlet fever.

November 24th: Schools reopened on Monday morning. Fever still very bad at the end of the three weeks and notice of two weeks further extension received. Three children have died since closing: forty away with or on account of scarlet fever.

Mr Heaton received invitation from managers to take the supervision of the girls' department.

1912

January 26th: Mr Kinton visited to arrange about a room
for lectures for women to be given on Tuesday
afternoons beginning February 6th. The old
'Baby Room' decided on as being most convenient.

    Fred M. smelt so badly on Tuesday afternoon
that I wrote again to his mother asking her to
wash his clothes. She came to school on Friday
morning very annoyed about it saying she always
sent him clean and that she should not send him
to this school again.

February 16th: Dr Wood examining several cases for eyesight.

February 23rd: Miss Bradley, Health Visitor, visited on Tuesday
and Thursday morning to see if any improvement
in children reported by doctor as having dirty
heads. Eveline C. so bad that she said must not
attend school again until cleaner.

    I sent a note to mother to this effect and the
same morning found Elsie was suffering from
scabies. Sent her home, too, advising advice from
a doctor.

March 15th: Dr Robinson visited on Monday morning to see
Eveline C. As she was much cleaner he allowed
her to stay, but said if she came dirty again I was
to send her home and notify him.

    Eveline C. very dirty on Friday afternoon. Sent
a note of warning to mother.

June 7th: Emily I. returned to school but head still in such
a filthy condition with sores and nits that sent her
home again.

June 28th: Chicken pox, measles and whooping cough on
the increase.

July 19th: Sent a note home on Wednesday morning to
                 mother of Mabel W. calling her attention to
                 child's head and saying she must not attend school
                 until clean. It was full of vermin.

September 27th: Sent Ethel B. and Edith O. home on Tuesday
                 suffering from sores on head caused by nits and
                 dirt. The latter had not been to school before since
                 the holidays.
                     On the same day sent Fred M. home for filth.
                 His clothes smelt so objectionable that he was
                 unfit to be in school.

October 4th: New brass studs put down in the floor of the
                 Drill Hall.

October 11th: Jack Fray knocked down by a bicycle while on
                 his way to school on Thursday morning and
                 badly hurt.

November 8th: Dr Fairer A.M.O. visited in the afternoon and
                 asked to see Lizzie L. and found her suffering from
                 general neglect; excluded her until 11th inst.
                     Her father brought her back 'to have it out with
                 the doctor' but he had gone. I gave him the notice
                 left for him.

December 20th: Mr Hyde brought me fifty tickets to give to the
                 poorest children in school to attend a tea on
                 December 27th.

1913

January 24th: Stanley Huckles fell off the end of a form on
                 Monday afternoon and made a tiny mark on his
                 head. Did not bleed. He seemed alright the next
                 morning, but in the afternoon his mother sent
                 word his head had begun to swell. I went to see

him and gave the mother, at once, a recommendation for the Cottage Hospital. She has taken him twice a day since for treatment and he is now going on well.

January 28th: Percy G. came with glasses today.

January 31st: Hilda Harris died on January 25th of diphtheria. Had been away from school since January 17th. Miss Jenkins (in whose class she was) was absent on Tuesday afternoon attending the funeral as a bearer.

February 21st: Violet Busson died on February 19th from dropsy. Had been away from school since June 6th owing first of all to bad eyes.

March 14th: I left school at three o'clock on Friday afternoon until after the Easter Holiday (by permission of the managers) to allow me to have a holiday in the Italian Riviera.

May 2nd: Miss Gertrude Willey resigned her position owing to her approaching marriage.

May 23rd: A holiday given on Friday afternoon to commemorate Empire Day.

June 6th: Attendance poor on Friday afternoon owing to rain. Several children had to go back home as they were wet through.

June 13th: John Gladwin returned to school after eight months absence with ringworm.

June 20th: A child, Jane P., died on Monday night. She was at school apparently alright in the morning but in the afternoon Ada T. brought word that she had 'stomach ache'.

The next morning a rumour circulated in the town that the child died through being hit on the head by her teacher because she asked for a drink of water. I visited the parents who seemed to have this idea. This was totally untrue as she neither asked for water nor was she struck.

Inquest, which her teacher attended and gave evidence, proved this, the finding being that the child died from a convulsive fit following a heat stroke. She was a quiet, undersized child and though nearly seven was no bigger than should have been at four.

July 18th: Dr Fairer and Miss Bradley visited on Tuesday afternoon to see Emily I. Emily came the next morning and as she had had her hair cut quite short and was much cleaner, I kept her at school. Miss Bradley came in later and said I had done quite right.

August 1st: Miss Clarke absent the whole of the week (by permission) to allow her to have a holiday in Switzerland.

October 17th: George B., who was excluded by School Medical Officer in April suffering from phthisis, returned to school on Monday afternoon. I sent him (with his teacher) to Dr Jenkins who said he must be sent home and mother take him for a thorough examination, and report the result to me. I called on her, and she promised to take him the next day.

October 24th: George B. returned to school on Wednesday morning. His mother took him to Dr Jenkins on Tuesday afternoon who thoroughly examined him and certified him fit for school.

December 5th: Reginald W. returned to school on Monday morning after an absence of thirteen and a half months, owing to ringworm.

Percentage of recorded deaths between
1879 and 1913 by disease

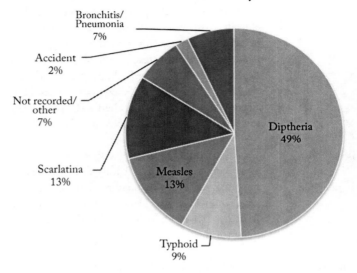

Between 1879 and 1913 the logbooks record many deaths
from diseases like diphtheria, measles and scarlatina.

Eight

The Great War, 1914–1919

The outbreak of the First World War on July 28th 1914 is a terrible time for everyone. Despite difficult conditions, the school is able to respond to an appeal to support the soldiers and sailors.

1914

January 12th: School Report on Nature Study by the Revd A. Thornley, Hinckley Infants' Council:

The programme in this school is full and varied and well suited to the infants. A definite nature lesson is given once a week and is connected with suitable drawing and modelling exercises. Conversation lessons are given more frequently, about three times a week. Records of 'First Things' are kept and bulbs grown and seeds germinated. I heard some exceedingly nice and appropriate recitations. The drawing and modelling is very pleasing.

January 23rd: Miss Bradley visited on Monday afternoon and excluded Edna S. and Reginald W. as hairs taken from head and microscopically examined found to be still infected with ringworm.

Emily I. and Elsie C. further excluded for a week by Dr Fairer for dirty and sore heads.

February 13th: Received a Chronic Disease Register.

February 20th: Miss Elsie Moore in school on Tuesday morning
to listen to a nature lesson, and Mr Millington
and Mr Lakey on Friday afternoon to enquire
into attendances of Elsie C., Emily I. and
Amy C. prior to issuing summons for time they
were excluded by Dr Fairer on account of nits
and sore heads.

March 6th: Instead of two last lessons on Monday afternoon,
Miss Elton came to school and talked to the
children about India and her children, illustrating
her talk with many curious things they make and
use. Children most interested.

     Evelyn C. very dirty and untidy again. I wrote
to her mother calling her attention to this, but
there is very little improvement.

May 4th: Report on boys' department:

     Guards are needed for two of the stoves. Some of the boys
     are rather untidy in appearance. Greater insistence on
     habits of cleanliness, attitude and concentration would be
     an improvement.

May 22nd: Excluded Ann W. from school until after the
Whitsuntide Holidays with a verminous and sore
head. I visited the mother and advised her to have
the child's hair cut short but this she refused to do.

June 17th: Admitted boy (Ed Davies) eight years old last
March. Does not know his letters. Been attending
private school in Leicester for a short time.
Mother said boy is 'very delicate'.

July 3rd: Sent in list, as requested, of mentally backward
children (three) and mentally deficient (one) to
Dr Robinson.

July 19th: Attendance worse each day. Only 286 present on Thursday. The correspondent received notice the same evening that owing to the prevalence of mumps and whooping cough this department must be closed at once. The children sent home accordingly at 9 o'clock on Friday morning until after the August Holidays.

July 31st: Mr Heaton writes: 'Under ordinary circumstances I was to have finished with August (age sixty-five). As the matter of the re-arrangement of the departments is not completed I have had a letter from the Correspondent expressing the unanimous wish of the managers that I would continue a little longer. Accepted the invitation.'

September 4th: Reopened school on Tuesday morning.

September 18th: Miss Bradley in school on Thursday to examine ringworm cases. At my request she inspected the heads of Lizzie and Doris P. as they are in a verminous condition and no improvement after two notes to mother from me. I wrote again and warned her of the consequences unless she attended to them.

October 16th: Miss Bradley visited on Thursday afternoon. She spoke to several children about having their clothes pinned instead of buttoned.

October 23rd: Miss Bradley visited on Tuesday morning and carefully examined each child's head as to cleanliness. Sent out printed directions as to treatment where she found nits.

November 20th: Edna I., admitted October 7th, made seven attendances and been absent since, reported had a bad foot, returned on Tuesday afternoon

but I found she had an infectious skin disease.
Sent her and George P., who I suspected of having
the same disease, to Dr Jenkins, who certified
them as having scabies and advised that all
children from the same houses be sent home.

December 4th: Sent in to Director, as requested, names and
addresses of children whose fathers are or have
been on active service. Eight in this department.

1915

January 15th: School reopened on Monday morning.
Reginald W. returned after nearly three years
absence owing to ringworm.

January 29th: Today closes my period of service; retired.
W. Heaton.

February 26th: On account of the length of time taken to
assemble the children and march them in, have
adopted a different system this week which bids
to shorten the time this absorbs and is conducive
to better order. The children move in double files
instead of going individually.

    The introduction of a minute or two
voice-training is having a good effect upon the
singing during the opening exercises.

March 5th: During the week have commenced the use of
'observation charts'.

April 16th: Yesterday the school nurse, Miss Bradley, called and
asked for our co-operation in promoting cleanliness
among the children. This was promised. I spoke to
the teachers and requested closer supervision of
dirty children. This morning spoke to the children
on the matter.

April 19th: Revd A. Thornley MA, the Nature Study Instructor for the Authority, visited the junior department this afternoon. He saw the work of the various classes in drawing from nature in crayon. He was informed that compilation of observation charts has been introduced and that the children were being interested in rearing living things. Mr Thornley expressed his satisfaction that the scheme, simple and elementary as it was, was on the right lines.

April 30th: There has been a sharp outbreak of measles during the week, no less than twenty-three cases have occurred.

May 14th: The correspondent received notice that owing to the prevalence of measles this department must be closed at once. The children accordingly sent home until further notice.

     An Empire Day appeal to children for pennies with which to provide small comforts for the soldiers and sailors realised 18*s* 7*d*, the number of contributions being 148. A pretty illuminated certificate will be presented to each contribution.

In 1915, an Empire Day appeal to children for pennies with which to provide small comforts for the soldiers and sailors realised 18*s* 7*d*. A certificate was presented to each child who made a contribution.

June 25th: Schools reopened on Monday morning after being closed for five and a half weeks owing to a severe epidemic of measles.

June 28th: A determined effort is being made to overcome the habit of coming to school dirty and untidy on the part of many of the children. The parents are greatly to blame for this.

July 16th: On Monday morning I found Nellie J. in the junior department rushing about the school and screaming like a mad child because she couldn't find another little girl. I took her to a seat and talked to her and after a time she got quiet and went to her class.

In the afternoon, on going out of school, the mother waylaid and abused me, using threatening and very bad language 'for slapping her child', a thing I did not do. She wouldn't listen to me but kept on shouting so I left her.

July 23rd: Miss Bradley visited on Thursday afternoon for her usual fortnightly inspection of ringworms.

July 30th: Miss Abell resigned her position as Assistant Mistress on Friday afternoon. Going to be married.

September 17th: Dr Robinson and Miss Bradley visited on Thursday afternoon to examine for ringworm and advise mothers as to treatment: excluded two children with impetigo.

October 1st: Miss Ingram informed me on Monday afternoon that 2s had been taken out of her box (Soldiers Fund) at dinnertime although it was locked up, and 2½s the week before. Found out that Geoffrey G. had had the money and on his own confession had spent it on sweets. I wrote to the mother who sent 1s to the fund out of his money box as a punishment.

October 8th: Miss Perkins, on the occasion of her marriage, granted the weeks holiday.

October 15th: Have forbidden the G. boys to come into the classroom at dinnertime as no matter how they are warned, they will get into mischief; nothing is safe from their interference.

November 26th: Edna I. came back on Tuesday afternoon after nearly fifteen months absence; suffered from scabies part of the time.

December 2nd: This school has for the second time sent a contribution to the Overseas Club Soldiers and Sailors Comfort Fund, this time of 19s. Throughout the whole of this year, the scholars have been contributing to the Relief of Distress in Belgium.

1916

January 14th: Schools reopened on Monday morning. Seven cases of measles, one of scarlet fever and two of ringworm reported.

February 11th: Have introduced slates in the lower classes for fear of shortage of paper.

March 3rd: A most trying week for both children and teachers. There has been no proper play interval for nearly a fortnight, the playground having been heaped with snow or drowned in slush.

March 24th: Mrs Summers' husband has the German measles and the Medical Officer has excluded her from school for twenty days.

April 7th: On Thursday afternoon Sister Bunyan, who has been nursing in India, came in and talked to the children about the children in that country and how they are faring in the war.

The keys of cupboards in the Drill Hall and stock cupboard taken away on Thursday and cannot be traced. Tom T. is credited with the theft but denies all knowledge of them. Mrs T. came to see me on Friday afternoon about other things he had taken and she took him to the police station. He said he had sold the keys to a man for a half penny. A policeman went with the boy to this man who gave them to him.

April 14th: Tom T. (aged six) came back after school on Thursday afternoon and stole 2½s out of teachers' apron pockets. Opened lid of large table and unfastened parcel of flags which were found in the cap room then went to the private room and emptied bags, boxes and ambulance bandages &c. about the room. Am unable to say what damage has been done to these.

The superintendent of police sent Sergeant Maddocks to see havoc wrought, who thought the best plan would be to take the boy to his father, which he did. In the afternoon his father brought him to school and returned a roll of bandages. Said he had punished him in all ways and didn't know what to do. The child, though bright in other ways, doesn't seem to understand and certainly has no fear.

May 5th: This afternoon during the last lesson we assembled for the celebration of the tercentenary of Shakespeare's death. Boys in Classes One, Two, Three and Four recited short poems from the plays and selections from one or two scenes from plays; a song was rendered also.

May 17th: Ernest Simpkin went to be medically examined as to his fitness for military service; was absent all day.

May 26th: A half-holiday given on Wednesday afternoon
              to commemorate Empire Day. All lessons in the
              morning on the subject of Empire. During the
              last lesson a modest celebration of this anniversary
              was indulged in. Suitable songs were sung and
              recitations done. The National Anthem was sung
              and the flag saluted.

              Miss Bradley visited on Thursday afternoon to
              see the ringworm cases. Stanley M. certified by
              Dr Jenkins as fit for school after fourteen months
              absence caused by this disease.

              Sarah M. excluded by Dr Jenkins for enlarged
              glands owing to nits.

July 28th: A little boy, Fred Ashton, died from effects
              of measles.

July 31st: This afternoon the boys' school passed (as a
              separate department) out of existence. Classes
              one to four inclusive have been drafted to a
              new boys' school which has taken the place of
              the Upper Mixed School. Infants' department

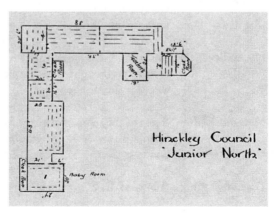

In 1916 the town was divided into north and south divisions.
The school was renamed Hinckley Council Junior North and
Hinckley Council Junior South. This plan shows the desk
arrangements in the Hinckley Council Junior North School.

reorganised as two junior departments consisting
of all children under nine on December 31st.
The town has been divided into north and south
divisions for this purpose. Children from the
north are placed in the senior infants' and boys'
department and from the south in the girls'.
The junior department of infants is to be used
as the girls' department. The teachers have been
allotted classes in the new boys', infants' and girls'
schools respectively.

October 2nd: £2 wrong in salaries and unable to find where.
Cheques seemingly alright: on going through the
figures found £1 short in July 28th payment and
another £1 short at end of quarter. I am the loser.

October 4th: Decided on going through registers that all classes
must be rearranged and put on a uniform footing
– sixty in a class.

October 20th: Not one of the rooms swept on Wednesday night
in either department. Windows not darkened.
Caretaker said could not get round before
lighting up time.

November 13th: Three children returned after ringworm. Doctor's
certificates brought. One, Stanley J., has been
away for fourteen months.

November 16th: Some of the rooms not swept for two days.
Schools in a very dirty condition. No blinds to the
windows the excuse.

December 8th: Allowed Mrs Summers to leave school at
three o'clock as her husband is going back to
his regiment.

December 11th: Mr Kiddle informed me that it had been decided,
owing to lighting difficulties in connection with

cleaning, that until further notice schools to close
at twelve o'clock morning and three thirty in
the afternoon.

1917

January 9th: Two cases of scarlet fever reported.

January 15th: Mrs Burgess unable to begin work this week as her husband is home from the front.

March 1st: Schools to close in the afternoon from this date at the ordinary time – quarter past four.

March 6th: Received 40lbs of Plasticine from Midland Educational Company.

April 17th: Miss Bott called up as a VAD nurse on 12th April.

May 2nd: Received circular from office concerning shortage and waste of food. Each child copied it from blackboard and took it home. Lessons are frequently given in this subject and have been for a long time.

June 6th: Miss Bradley visited each class and tested each child with defective eyesight.

September 6th: Mr Whatmore finds that children from this department and the south work subtraction by a different method. The difference is we subtract from ten and add unit, in the south they add ten and unit together and then subtract. He asks is it possible to work uniformly.

September 11th: Received a circular letter asking children to collect horse chestnuts. Children have responded well to this appeal.

September 17th: Miss Lucas informs me that two of her brothers had measles, but that she left home at once. I consulted Dr Jenkins who advised me to exclude her from school and to write to Dr Robinson. This I did and received reply that she must not return to school for three weeks, nor go home until house certified free from infection by the Sanitary Authority.

October 22nd: Dr Jenkins, Medical Officer of Health, and Mrs Abbott visited in the afternoon to inspect lavatory accommodation. Found all water turned off over the basins. Only supply obtained from the pump in one of the cloakrooms.

November 2nd: Mrs Summers absent until ten o'clock – her husband arrived unexpectedly from France.

November 30th: Schools very dirty – only swept once during the week owing to lighting restrictions.

December 21st: Schools closed on Friday afternoon for the usual Christmas Holidays.

1918

January 11th: Mr H. Kiddle visited – the question of fire guards discussed as there are two stoves quite unprotected.

January 25th: Miss Burgess away by permission all day on Thursday and Friday; husband home from France.

March 8th: Attendance very poor. Measles on the increase. Schools closed on Wednesday morning by order of the Chief Medical Officer until March 25th.
    During the closing of the schools all the teachers assisted at the Council Offices with Food Cards and visited schools in Leicester.

April 12th: Schools reopened on Tuesday morning with a
                    good attendance: only fifteen children away owing
                    to measles.

April 19th: Attendance irregular all week. Children in several
                    cases getting revised meal tickets. Two fresh cases
                    of measles.
                        Miss Lucas absent by permission on Wednesday
                    afternoon to attend a service at Barwell for soldiers
                    killed in the war. Has lost a brother.

May 31st: Mr Martin visited in the afternoon to talk over
                    the sanitary arrangements – still no water for
                    children to wash, except at the pump.

June 28th: I was not at school on Thursday afternoon from
                    three o'clock until five past four, as I was attending
                    a meeting to arrange about means of raising
                    money for the Prisoners of War in Germany Fund.

July 5th: Miss A. Lucas left school on Monday morning
                    at half past eleven ill (influenza). Many children
                    away from the same cause and several taken
                    suddenly ill in school and had to go home.

July 12th: Attendance poor, especially towards the end of
                    the week. Only 307 present on Friday morning.
                    Influenza the cause.

July 19th: Attendance bad all the week. Many children
                    returned after influenza but fresh ones away.

October 4th: Sent notes to parents whose children are attending
                    irregularly. Answers containing excuses received in
                    most cases.
                        Sent a letter to the managers asking for advice
                    as to admitting a five-year-old who will never walk
                    as her legs are turned the wrong way – her mother
                    (Mrs T.) says nothing can be done for her.

October 25th: Attendance good until Thursday – poor since. Influenza and colds the principal cause.

November 8th: Sent for Mrs T. to bring her little girl to school on Monday morning and, as she does not go out to work, she arranged to come each morning at playtime to attend to her.

    Directly the registers were marked Mr Kiddle brought a notice from Dr Robinson to close the school at once on account of influenza, until 16th November. Children sent home and attendances cancelled.

December 13th: Schools reopened on Monday morning with a very fair attendance: 318 present. Dr Jenkins Certified Leah M. as fit to attend school. She has been away for a year suffering with scabies.

Often mistaken for a bell tower, this is actually a ventilation shaft for the air circulation system around the school. Early plans show a large fan installed under the hall floor, but whether this was ever built or how it was intended to be powered is unknown.

1919

January 10th: Mrs Summers absent by permission on Wednesday afternoon and the rest of the week, husband home from Cologne.

Mrs T. did not come to attend to her child at playtime, as arranged, on Thursday nor again on Friday. When I sent for her she was very angry and said she should not send her again as she couldn't come to see to her. Does not go to work.

February 14th: Have been to see Mrs T. who was fetched from a neighbour's house where she said she was cleaning. She says she cannot come to attend to Catherine at playtime and shall not send her to school this winter. I found the child at half past ten on a bitterly cold frosty morning with only a little chemise on. She said she was cold, but the mother made very light of her not being dressed and said, 'She isn't cold.' The house was altogether dirty and miserable.

February 21st: Have sent from the children and staff £3 14*s* to St Dunstan's Hostel. Part of this money was collected before the Armistice was signed to send cigarettes &c. to the soldiers. After a talk with the children they decided they would add to it and send it to the Blinded Soldiers.

March 7th: Attendance poor on Friday morning: excuse was 'doing errands'.

March 21st: Notice received this morning that the Education Year shall henceforth correspond with the Registration Year – April 1st to March 31st.

April 14th: Four teachers away all week. Correspondent telephoned to the office on Monday and help promised, but so far none come.

April 18th: A case of spotted fever reported. The boy has been away from school since March 31st suffering from influenza and bronchitis. Removed to Leicester Isolation Hospital.

Received notice that in future children under five years of age can only be admitted at the commencement of the school year in April.

May 23rd: A holiday given on Friday afternoon to commemorate Empire Day. Lessons given in the morning bearing on the subject.

June 6th: Miss Lucas away all day Wednesday suffering from gnat bites.

June 20th: Punished twelve boys for throwing stones on going out of school on Wednesday afternoon: north and south junior departments taking sides and the big boys joining in.

June 27th: A holiday given on Friday afternoon by permission of the managers, as five girls from the girls' school had gained a County Scholarship.

July 4th: Attendance irregular. Mothers complain that the children will not come in early at night, and consequently a difficult matter to get them up in time for school in the morning.

July 18th: Took Irene P. and Leah M. to the doctor as I was not satisfied about having them in school: have excluded both, the former for mumps and the latter for an infectious skin disease.

The Chairman visited on Thursday morning to propose we assemble as usual on Friday morning and after a talk on Thanksgiving, singing hymns &c. we dismiss for the day as a Peace Holiday. This was done.

August 1st: Evelyn Cheshire sent by her teacher on Thursday morning to ask why Ada Weaver was away from school. The dog bit her on her leg and her mother took her at once to the doctor who cauterized

it and advised her to inform them at the police
station. Has been in school since and going
on alright.

September 5th: During playtime in the afternoon Nora Beasley
had a finger cut rather badly by pushing up against
William Simpson who had an open jackknife in his
hand. Have taken charge of it until someone from
his home comes for it as I consider it too dangerous
a weapon for him to have.

   A case of scarlet fever and one of chicken pox
reported.

October 3rd: War Savings Accounts sent in for audit and closed.
During the three years £358 subscribed, 447
certificates purchased and £11 11s 6d withdrawn.

   Mrs Warner and Mrs Summers resigned
their position as un-certificated assistants on
September 30th: the latter after nearly twenty
years' of service. Husbands want them at home.

October 10th: Miss Beardmore, the new school nurse, visited
on Wednesday and Thursday afternoon and
examined each child as to cleanliness. A few
children with nits and three with nits and
vermin. Said was very satisfied.

October 17th: On Friday morning punished Alfred Hoult,
Harry Carter, Stanley Orton, Charles Wykes,
Tom Armstrong, Alex Moore and Sam Blower for
throwing stones.

   In the afternoon, Tom Mason told his teacher
that he had swallowed his pencil, a small slate one.
Have informed his father.

October 24th: Schools closed on Friday afternoon for the October
Break, which the managers have extended three
extra days in place of an extension of the August
Holiday as a Peace Holiday.

November 7th: Miss Ruscoe, the drill instructress, visited on Wednesday afternoon and was most helpful to the teachers. She, at their request, kindly took a class for drill and dancing.

November 21st: Children sent home on Monday morning at 9.45 as there were no stoves going and school too cold to work in. Attendances cancelled. The heating has been unsatisfactory for some time owing to illness of caretaker. Many days no stoves going in Classrooms Two and Three: teachers complaining of bad colds in consequence.

Hinckley Board School was originally organised in three separate departments, infants', junior boys' and junior girls', each with its own head teacher and logbook. The girls' entrance is still clearly visible but no longer used.

November 28th: Stoves a trouble all the week. The man does his best but morning after morning two or three stoves out.

December 12th: Children sent home on Monday morning, no fires going and again on Thursday. School too cold for children to work. Attendance cancelled at 10 o'clock. We, the staff, stayed till nearly twelve o'clock trying to get them to go and succeeded in lighting three but one of these out in the afternoon. Schools worked with difficulty all the week. Man says unable to do the work without help.

Messrs Moore, Davenport, Goode and H. Kiddle visited on Tuesday morning to consider what could be done. A fresh man began on Wednesday but results no better if as good, though he moves about quicker.

December 19th: A struggle to keep going on Monday and Tuesday owing to difficulty with stoves. Both mornings most of them out and had to light them ourselves. Had a straight talk with the man and has managed better since.

Nine

Age of Reform, 1920–1942

Following the First World War, education began to see a number of reforms. Health visitors, dental practitioners, opticians and Medical Officers are becoming regular visitors to the school. Reorganisation saw a name change to Albert Road County Primary School.

1920

January 9th: All rooms clean and warm. A new stove put in large classroom.

January 30th: Dr Murray came in at half past ten on Monday morning to begin the Medical Inspection. Inspection lasted for the three following days.

February 6th: As an outcome of the Medical Inspection, three children have had operations for adenoids and tonsils.

February 13th: Mr Payne and Mr H. Kiddle visited on Tuesday morning and Miss Freeman, Health Visitor, on Thursday, when she examined each child in Standard One and Two as to cleanliness.

Children with defective eyesight attended at the old Town Hall on Friday afternoon to see Dr Murray.

February 27th: Most of the parents of children with defective eyesight have obtained spectacles for them.

March 5th: I took three children to the school clinic on Wednesday morning; one with ringworm, one with an abscess on his head and the other with a sore ear. All received treatment.

    Nine children out of twelve that Dr Musson prescribed spectacles have got them.

March 12th: Attendance fallen off due to the prevalence of coughs and colds amongst the children. Another case of whooping cough reported.

    The school dentist present the whole of Tuesday and Wednesday morning, and all day on Thursday and Friday, 'repairing' teeth. A notice sent to parents for permission to do this.

March 26th: School dentist in school extracting teeth on Monday, Tuesday and Thursday, and workmen in and out all the week in connection with the new heating apparatus.

March 31st: A lock in a cupboard forced open between Friday night and Monday morning and twenty-one pencils missing.

    Work carried on with difficulty as workmen are in the schools all the time and one part of Standard Two cannot be used.

For the rest of this term, the logbook reported major disruption due to building work being carried out in the school. Many references to the problems caused but no specific details of what was being done.

April 13th: Unable to open school after the Easter Holidays as workmen were putting in hot water pipes. Children were sent home for another week.

April 19th: Schools still not ready. I explained the matter
                   to the children and sent them home for
                   another week.

April 30th: Reopened on Monday morning. Found the
                   schools in such a dirty condition that we had to
                   dust and tidy up before admitting children.

May 21st: Have been unable to adhere strictly to the
                   timetable as workmen have been in first one room
                   and then another and classes have had to move
                   about and do the best they could.

June 25th: On Tuesday morning Nellie Lovett slipped down
                   a hole in the floor, made by workmen, bruising
                   her leg and breaking the skin a little. Have asked
                   Mr Goodman to attend to it, but so far has not
                   done so.

July 9th: Forwarded from the children £1 1s 0d to
                   'Sunshine House', the home for blind babies.

September 10th: On Wednesday morning, at the clinic, Dr Murray,
                   at my request, medically examined Paul C. and
                   found him quite fit for school. His mother sent
                   a note that morning, after a week's absence,
                   saying he was not well and under the doctor,
                   which was not true. The boy said he had to mind
                   the baby and had not seen a doctor. Has only
                   made twenty-five attendances out of a possible
                   sixty-eight.

October 1st: The name of Catherine T. taken off the registers
                   by permission of Dr Robinson: has not attended
                   since January 10th 1919.

October 15th: Heating apparatus set going on Wednesday
                   morning, but schools so hot on Thursday that asked
                   the caretaker to let the fire out as he said he could

not regulate the heat. Classroom over 72°F and other rooms 68°F at nine o'clock and soon much higher, this had all the windows and doors open. W. Freer visited in the afternoon and said the heat could be regulated, and the next morning sent his son to take the temperature of each room and instruct caretaker.

October 22nd: Miss Ruscoe visited on Monday afternoon and had several classes in the playground to see them at physical exercises. Miss Freeman on Tuesday afternoon inspected Standard Two as to cleanliness and was in attendance with the doctor at the school clinic on Wednesday morning.

Schools closed for the usual two days break and three days extension on account of the schools being used for the Cottage Hospital Bazaar.

November 5th: Unable to open school on Monday morning as the furniture was in the playground and nothing ready. I interviewed the Chairman, who advised that the children be sent home for another day.

December 10th: Several fresh cases of mumps and chicken pox reported. Attendance very low on Friday morning, partly on account of hunters and foxhounds meeting in the town.

December 24th: Forwarded £2 2s 0d from the children to St Dunstan's Hostel for Blinded Soldiers and Sailors.

1921

February 4th: Medical Inspection on Monday, Tuesday and Wednesday: 157 children examined. Phyllis P. found to have a very bad heart and weak lungs. Must not drill or exert herself in any way; William W. very weak chest and delicate; Connie B. quite unfit to attend school yet and Dr Murray advised that she be kept in this department for another year as she is too weakly to cope with older girls. Several fresh cases of mumps and chicken pox, also one of scabies.

February 11th: Weighed and took height of all children medically examined and forwarded cards to the Chief Medical Officer.

February 25th: The school dentist in school Tuesday, Wednesday, Thursday and Friday examining and repairing teeth.
A half-holiday given on Thursday afternoon for the opening of the YMCA.

June 10th: Three children each brought a note on Friday morning saying they had not had any breakfast (father a miner). I provided them with some. Forwarded the case by request of Mr Hill as he had been asked to attend a meeting to deal with such cases.

June 17th: Miss Wix in school and inspected the work of the infants, taking special note of the backward children and getting particulars, as far as known, to cause.

June 24th: Provided dinner on Thursday, at the request of the parents, for three children. Mr Hill informed me in the afternoon that the Distress Committee would attend to necessitous cases in future.

July 22nd: Attendance very poor on Tuesday owing to a Baby Welfare Party at Leicester Grange.
Elsie Summers absent all next week, by permission, attending a vacation course at the Derby Training College in dancing, games, physical exercises and musical appreciation.

September 2nd: Mrs Antrobus in school on Thursday morning and looked carefully at each child to see if they had any suspicious spots on them.

Dr Murray also came in, in the afternoon,
to enquire if children suffering from enlarged
tonsils or adenoids had had them removed.
All except two had.

September 16th: Two children excluded by health visitor suffering
from impetigo.

On Friday afternoon, £1 1s 3d was missed
from a tin in Mrs Warner's cupboard. Upon
enquiry found that four boys had been taking
a few shillings at playtime each day during
the week, spending the money on fruit and
sweets. Informed parents who came to school
to investigate. One boy fetched 1s 9d that he
had hidden under a post, but so many untruths
told, decided a policeman should talk to the
boys. The superintendent came and spoke very
kindly to them. Afterwards he questioned each
separately, writing down what they told him,
and the case was left in his hands.

September 23rd: The boys who had the money from Mrs Warner's
cupboard were punished by their parents and the
money refunded.

September 30th: Attendance irregular all week – many children
having a half day to go to Barwell Wake.

On Thursday afternoon, after thirty-three years'
service, I resign the charge of this school.

October 3rd: I commenced duties as Headmistress of this
department. Held staff meeting at quarter past
four, when we decided to adopt the 'Mason'
method of teaching in the junior part of the
school and to use individual methods of work in
the infant part.

December 21st: The caretaker reported that the boiler had burst
during the night and that consequently he was

unable to heat the school. Reported the matter to the Correspondent. Owing to the excessive cold it was decided to close the school a day earlier.

1922

February 28th: A day's holiday was granted in commemoration of the Wedding of Princess Mary.

April 3rd: Mr Woodcock, the new Correspondent, visited the school.

June 22nd: In the afternoon a half-holiday was granted owing to the visit of HRH Princess Alice to Hinckley.

Reward medals for regular attendance continued long into the twentieth century.

November 20th: Extract from report by HM Inspectress Miss Wix:

Many of the children come from sadly sordid homes and the teachers' work here includes much beyond mere 'schooling'. Among the most important things these children will have to learn are neatness and cleanliness in words and person and gentleness both in manner and speech.

December 22nd: During the afternoon distributed Christmas gifts to the children and held a 'breaking up' concert.

1923

April 26th: School closed for the day – Wedding of HRH The Duke of York.

1924

January 25th: Roll: 321 – attendance poor owing to the prevalence of influenza.

July 1st: In connection with Education Week, Open Day was held in this department when the school was open to visitors. From quarter past three in the afternoon visitors were given a selection from the songs and dances learnt during the term.

October 17th: The whole school was closed for the day as the children from the senior department were visiting Wembley.

November 7th: Attendance this last week low owing to cases of various infectious diseases.

November 18th: Mrs Broadley sent word that her boy, Harry, had suddenly been taken to the Cottage Hospital and notified me a few days later that he had died from meningitis. The children in his class subscribed for flowers to be sent to his funeral.

November 21st: Miss Wix HMI called for particulars of the number of backward children in the school.

December 18th: Mr Kerslake HMI and Mr Brockington visited the school and held a conference with the head teachers concerning the proposed alteration of the four departments.

It was decided that this department should be purely an infant school with Standard One and that about 114 of the infants in the South School should be transferred to this school. At the same time Standard Three and Standard Two boys were to be transferred to the senior departments.

1925

January 30th: Attendance lower still – 74 per cent. Two cases of diphtheria, two of mumps, three of whooping cough and fifty of measles reported. Owing to the cases of diphtheria the school was stoved (fumigated) on Saturday morning.

February 6th: Seventy cases of measles reported. Attendance for the week 63 per cent.

February 12th: The school was closed for the afternoon to enable the teachers to visit Leicester and hear the President of the Board of Education (Lord Eustace Percy) speak on education.

April 21st: Miss Caves absent – attending three weeks course at Sheffield for teachers of backward children.

May 29th: The school was closed at twelve o'clock for the Whitsuntide Holidays. The Friday afternoon was granted in addition to the usual holiday as a 'merit' holiday for the exceptionally good attendance during the last month.

December 16th/17th: During the afternoon of these two days the school was 'open' to parents. The children sang and danced and there was an exhibition of raffia work, needlework and other handiwork. About eighty mothers attended. Most of the things which had been made were sold. The proceeds amounted to £2 5s, which went towards the school funds.

1926

February 16th: The school was closed in the afternoon for the usual half-holiday.

November 20th: Attendance for the past six weeks has been low – about 85 per cent – owing to an epidemic of mumps.

1927

January 11th: Reopened school after the Christmas Holidays. Roll: 408. School very crowded at the lower end, the three bottom classes having fifty-nine, fifty-eight and fifty-two children on roll respectively.

June 20th: Roll now 450. Attendance much improved.

October 24th: Heat on for the first time – heating apparatus had been out of order – often 40-50°F – in school.

1928

October 19th: The school was closed for the afternoon session – concert in palladium for Cottage Hospital.

1929

November 11th: Armistice Day. Special talks were given to the children, special hymns were sung and prayers read. The two minutes silence was observed.

1930

March 13th: A staff meeting was held at four o'clock when all the eleven members of the staff were present. Various important matters relating to the conduct of the school were discussed. It was definitely stated that canes, pointers and pencils should not be used for punishment and that corporal punishment should be in the hands of the head teacher only.

July 2nd: I was absent from school in the afternoon to attend the funeral of Miss Fellows, headmistress of the girls' department – with whom I had lived and worked for thirteen years.

October 31st: Sixty-four children accompanied by two teachers visited the Empire Fruit Exhibition at Leicester.

November 11th: Extract from Report by HMI Mr A. T. Kerslake:

Since the last report the staff has been increased and strengthened, but half of the ten classes still have fifty children each on the roll, and a rather large percentage of the scholars is, as usual, of a backward type.

1931

April 14th: Admitted forty-two children. Classes now over-crowded – sixty-two and sixty-three children in two lowest classes.

June 29th: Mrs Brown commenced duty. Mrs Brown, being a
                    widow, was eligible for a permanent position.

1932

April 5th: Roll: 622. Owing to the crowded condition of
                    the school, the managers had made arrangements
                    during the holiday for the hiring of a room in
                    the Primitive Methodist Schoolroom opposite.
                    Miss Bell was transferred there with her class of
                    fifty-two children.

September 8th: Received fifty tables and twenty-five chairs for use
                    in the Primitive Methodist Schoolroom.
                    Roll: 699.

1933

January 19th: 250 children absent suffering from influenza
                    and colds.

April 25th: An additional class was accommodated in
                    the large room of the Primitive Methodist
                    Schoolroom. Curtains were received from
                    Messrs Dale and Reeves and the room divided
                    into three parts. There are now five classes in the
                    P.M. Schoolroom.

December 20th: Mr Ritchie, Chief HMI, visited the school for a
                    short time. He advised that classes should no longer
                    be accommodated in the Primitive Methodist
                    Schoolroom but that accommodation should be
                    found for four classes in the senior girls' school.
                    The question was discussed with the headmistress
                    of the senior girls' school. She agreed to let us have
                    the use of four classrooms on the ground floor of
                    her department. Arrangements made accordingly.

Letter received by Head Teacher Miss Upson, dated
January 1st 1934, requesting School Report to be copied
into the logbook.

1934

January 1st: Copy of Report of Inspection on
December 19th 1933 by HMI Mr K. J. Ritchie:

Junior Mixed and Infant Department. The question
of accommodation in this department requires urgent
consideration. It has not been completely relieved by
the opening of the Westfield Council Junior Mixed
and Infants School. There are at present 630 on books
with a further 60 children expected. The recognised
accommodation of the building is 373. Three classes of
infants are accommodated in two rooms of the Primitive
Methodist Schoolroom adjoining.

The upstairs rooms are obviously unsuited for infants, as the only access is up a steep stone stairs, the handrail of which is too high for infants to use.

In the adjacent senior girls' department there are four rooms vacant, and it appears possible to use these temporarily rather than pay rent for very indifferent temporary premises.

It is obvious that there exists a serious deficiency in accommodation for juniors and infants; the provision of more demands urgent consideration and systematic planning for the future. As it is, the position is growing worse rather than better.

January 9th: *The logbook discusses in detail the problems of accommodating the large number of pupils in the school. Once again classes are transferred to the Primitive Methodist Schoolrooms and classes shuffled between the infant and senior schools.*

March 29th: Electric light has been fitted in this department during the past week.

September 10th: Important structural alterations had been made to the school during the holidays. Among other things one classroom had been turned into a cloakroom, the old Board Room had been made into a classroom and the end classroom had been altered into a staffroom. New doors, new washbowls &c. had been installed and doors from the various classrooms had been made to open on to a veranda.

October 1st: New milk scheme – ⅓ pint bottles reduced from 1*d* to ½*d* each.

November 29th: School closed for the day in accordance with the wishes of the King on the occasion of the Wedding of HRH the Duke of Kent and Princess Marina of Greece.

1935

March 14th: Miss Goodman, representative of the Milk
Marketing Board, visited the school and talked to
the children on the value of milk.

May 6th: Silver Jubilee of His Majesty, the King. The school
was closed for two days. On the afternoon of
May 6th, a children's fancy dress parade and school
sports took place in Richmond Park. Afterwards a
tea was given to the children in the day schools of the
town. Each child was presented with a jubilee mug.

May 23rd: Last day of occupation of Primitive Methodist
Schoolroom. These premises have been occupied
by this school since April 5th 1932. They have
been used to accommodate a varying number
of children owing to the crowded conditions of
the school.

May 27th: The school is now called Albert Road County
Primary School. The junior classes are housed
in the old 'Junior North' building and the infant
classes in the former 'Junior South'.

On May 27th 1935, the school was renamed Albert Road
County Primary School. A school tie and cap were
also available.

September 3rd: During the holidays, further structural alterations had been made to the school. In the infant section of the school the cloakroom had been considerably enlarged, four new wash bowls inserted and a new floor laid. A roof light had also been inserted at the far end of the large room. Two new floors had been laid in the cloakrooms of the junior section of the school and this section had been painted and decorated internally.

The recommended alterations and improvements to the whole of the school building which were commenced during August 1934 were now completed. Thus the school has been remodelled and an out-of-date building, containing out-of-date furniture, has now been brought in line with the modern requirements of education.

September 13th: Visit of demonstration showing health and cleanliness film. The older junior children saw the film.

September 18th: Miss Turner, organiser for backward classes, visited the school.

November 6th: School closed for the day in accordance with the wishes of the King on the occasion of the marriage of the Duke of Gloucester.

November 14th: General Election. School used as a polling booth and consequently closed for the day.

1936

January 28th: The school was closed for the day on the occasion of the funeral of King George V.

April 30th: Miss Atherton (Milk Publicity Council) spoke to the children on the value of milk.

September 1st: New piano received during holidays.

December 22nd: An open day for parents was held. About 200 parents visited the school and saw the work of the children.

1937

January 15th: Attendance this week very low (79 per cent) owing to influenza epidemic.

March 11th: Attendance abnormally low – 55 per cent – 300 present out of 544. Exceptionally heavy fall of snow.

May 11th/ 12th/13th: School closed for holiday granted on the occasion of the coronation of their Majesties King George VI and Queen Elizabeth. Tea given to all school children in the day schools of the town.

June 29th: The managers decided to forward some suggestions to the Leicestershire County Council concerning the safety of the school children on entering and leaving the school when the new bypass road along the Holliers Walk side of the building is completed.

November 3rd: Supply of milk (under Milk Scheme for Schools) now obtained from Hinckley Co-operative Society.

November 11th: Armistice Day. Vernon Bartlett's 'Message to Schools' (supplied by LEA) was read to the older children and the two minutes' silence observed.

1938

September 27th: Received notice to forward to LEA number of children residing more than ten minutes' walk away from the school. (ARP)

September 28th: Received sample gas masks and instructed to demonstrate use of same to all children. (ARP)

1939

September 3rd: Outbreak of war.

October 25th: School reopened for first time since mid-summer holidays.

 The lateness of the opening was due to the time taken in making preparations for the safety of the children during an air raid. The whole of the Infant Department of the school had been made into a shelter for the protection of the children and consequently it was decided that this department was not suitable for school use by the children. External premises were therefore decided upon and the Primitive Methodist Schoolroom, which had formally been used by this school, was once more obtained for use. All lower infant classes together with the special class were transferred to this building.

 Evacuees: forty-four evacuees from Alum Rock Junior and Infant School, Birmingham, were admitted to the school. Two teachers accompanied the children.

November 1st: The Director of Education visited the school and inspected the shelters. (ARP)

November 20th: Afternoon session altered to finish earlier owing to the lighting restrictions.

1940

January 19th: Mr Butler, Organiser of Leicestershire and Rutland Band of Hope Union, visited the school and addressed older children on the hygiene of food and drink.

April 15th: Mr Bennet, having been called up to serve with His Majesty's Forces, ceased duty (temporarily) on the staff of the school.

April 17th: Mr Chappell, also having been called up to serve with His Majesty's Forces, ceased duty temporarily.

September 17th: Mr Royle, HMI visited the school for a short time in the afternoon regarding the question of day nurseries for children of women munitions workers. None necessary in Hinckley.

November 12th: During the past few weeks have admitted about sixty evacuees – the majority from London.

November 15th: Abnormally low attendance owing to an air raid the previous night.

November 28th: Admitted twenty-five evacuated children from Bloomsbury Road School, Birmingham.

December 5th: Mrs Turk absent. House bombed and completely demolished.

December 16th: Evacuees: Birmingham fifty-two, Coventry twenty-three, London forty-two – total 117.

1941

February 27th: Children's gas masks examined by ARP wardens.

March 14th: The Lord Mayor and Lady Mayoress of Birmingham visited the school and spoke to evacuated children who were assembled here from the various schools in Hinckley.

April 9th: Attendance depleted owing to air raid in district previous night.

April 28th: Diphtheria immunisation – preliminary treatment: 150 children immunised by Dr Shirlaw.

May 19th: Mrs Power (London) absent. Suffering from serious injuries due to enemy action.

May 26th: Diphtheria immunisation – second inspection.

June 19th: Acting on instructions received by me from the Education Committee, a boy was punished for stealing keys from two air-raid shelters in the town. I administered corporal punishment, several strokes of the cane being given.

November 21st: Mrs Chappell absent – husband home on leave.

December 10th: All children listened to a talk given by a police sergeant on 'Safety First'.

1942

January 1st: Attended a meeting in the County Rooms, Leicester, regarding School Dinner Scheme.

October 25th: Owing to ill health I ceased duty as headmistress of this school.

Ten

Post-1942

Following the resignation of Miss Upson, Mr Alec Donald Stanley is appointed as headmaster. Under his leadership the school begins to develop a reputation for musical and sporting excellence, new educational ideas are introduced and the school develops the curriculum beyond the classroom.

Swimming lessons at the local swimming pool commence in May 1944 when the head teacher records: 'Clifford Lurch fell in the deep end. The headteacher was obliged to jump in and fetch him out. There were no ill effects.'

On January 30th 1945 the school introduced school dinners. Approximately 100 children and 6 staff stayed to eat a daily cooked meal.

On January 30th 1945 the school introduced school dinners: 'Approximately 100 children and 6 staff stay to dinner daily. Two members of staff are on duty. The headteacher is present for the greater part of most meals or at least once per week for the whole time.'

During May 1945 the school took part in the Victory in Europe Celebrations. The children were given a tea and each child was given a newly minted shilling.

In October of the same year, a tragedy occurred in the playground. Two boys crossing the playground were hit by the flagpole which blew down in a sudden gust of wind. The headteacher records: 'It is great regret that I record that Anthony Russell (age ten years) subsequently died of his injuries.'

For the Coronation of her Majesty Queen Elizabeth II, June 2nd 1953, children were given an additional holiday, a mug and a packet of sweets. Some members of staff helped with the organisation of sports and a fancy dress parade in the town.

In November 1962 teachers attended a meeting about the Augmented Roman Alphabet. This will later become known as the Initial Teaching Alphabet (ITA), a method of teaching which the school will pioneer.

Over the following years the school developed an international reputation for its teaching methods, curriculum development and the implementation of new educational ideas under the 'Leicestershire Experiment'.

sally gœs ʃhoppiŋ

wun dæ sally's muᴣher sed, "cum on, wɛɛ hav tω gœ ʃhoppiŋ bɛɛfœr yω gœ tω scωl."
thæ waukd tω ᴣhe grœsers tω bie sum orænjes and ʃhωgar.
then sally went to scωl and muᴣher went hœm.

In November 1962 the school introduced the Initial Teaching Alphabet (ITA). One of the first schools in the country to do so, the alphabet was based on a phonetic alphabet developed by Sir James Pitman. The intention was to make reading more easily accessible to younger children. The system was eventually discontinued in 1982. (Illustration © Julie Elverstone, 2013)

Visitors to the school include representatives from the USA, the Irish Free State, Scotland, Johannesburg, Gambia and Bahrain, as well as visits from the Directors of Education and leading educationalists from the Isle of Wight, London, Yorkshire, Lancashire, Leeds, Cambridge, Lincolnshire, Chesterfield, London, Coventry, Worcester, Hereford, Loughborough and Birmingham. More than thirty different visits are recorded.

In 1967 residential visits were introduced. Children were taken to field study centres at Woodchester Park, Hafod Meurig, Foxton and Fairbourne.

On June 27th 1969, Mr R.D. Brooks is appointed head teacher.

Parents are encouraged to play a greater part in school life with the formation of the Albert Road Parent Teacher Association on October 1st 1970. Almost immediately parents petition for improved toilet facilities for the children, which results in the replacement of the old toilet block by three mobile units.

The temporary nature of the new toilets is the result of the announcement that Albert Road School is to be replaced by a new school and land has been purchased for the purpose. The PTA begins fundraising to build a swimming pool in the new school and by 1973 has raised £2,000.

Excitement raised by the prospect of a new school is cut short in January 1974. 'Large cut-backs in local authority spending mean the new school is to be shelved. As a replacement building it has no priority and therefore will not now be commenced. Appeal to the director has failed. Money raised for the swimming pool is to be spent on a new school library and audio visual equipment.'

The school celebrated its centenary in 1978. An exhibition and pageant was organised in school and children took part in the Hinckley Carnival Procession. In the same year, the local authority confirmed that the school building is not to be replaced. Albert Road School is to continue in the old building 'for a long time yet'.

On January 1st 1985 the school changes its name to Holliers Walk Primary School. It was decided that the uniform should be predominately grey with a burgundy jumper or sweatshirt. The jumper and sweatshirt should carry the new school name and a school logo, the hansom cab.

On December 20th 1987 the school logbook is discontinued.

***

Today, as we approach the 150th anniversary of the 1870 Education Act, no matter what educational thinking changes the teaching and delivery of the school curriculum; no matter how the building continues to be shaped and developed, the fact remains that the pupils, both past and present, have every right to look back to their heritage and proudly boast that they were taught in a Victorian School in Leicestershire.

On January 1st 1985 the school changed its name to Holliers Walk Primary School, the name by which it is still known today.

Lightning Source UK Ltd.
Milton Keynes UK
UKOW04f0600130314

228050UK00001B/1/P